Sufi Inayat Khan was born in Baroda, India, into a family of musicians. After establishing himself at an early age as a master musician, he worked for the revival of interest in the spiritual heritage of Indian music. He received initiation from his Sufi teacher and trained in the four major Indian schools of Sufism: Chishti, Naqshibandi, Qadiri, and Suhrawardi. When his training was completed, he left India for the West, where he lectured and traveled throughout Europe and America and founded the International Sufi Movement. His writings have touched the lives of many who welcome the breadth and wholeness of his vision, and who are inspired by his respect for every human ideal.

# The Development
of
# Spiritual Healing

## INAYAT KHAN

Sufi Publishing
An Imprint of Hunter House Publishers

Reprinted from
The Sufi Message of Hazrat Inayat Khan

First published by Barrie & Rockliff, 1961

Second publication by Sufi Publishing Company, Ltd.,
1974
This edition published by Hunter House Inc.
© 1988, 1974, 1961 International Headquarters of the Sufi
Movement
Geneva, Switzerland
Cover design and special setting for this edition
© 1988 Hunter House Inc., Publishers
PO Box 847, Claremont, CA 91711, U.S.A.

Library of Congress Catalog Card Number 87-92057
ISBN 0-89793-060-6

Cover design by Virginia M. Fontana
Manufactured in the United States of America

9 8 7 6 5 4 3 2    Fourth edition

# Contents

# Part
# 1

# Health

ILLNESS is an inharmony, either physical inharmony or mental inharmony, the one acts upon the other. What causes inharmony? The lack of tone and rhythm. How can it be interpreted in physical terminology? Prana, or life, or energy is the tone; circulation, regularity is the rhythm, regularity in the beatings of the head, of the pulse and the circulation of the blood through the veins. In physical terms the lack of circulation means congestion; and the lack of Prana, or life, or energy means weakness. These two conditions attract illness and are the cause of illness. In mental terms the rhythm is the action of the mind, whether the mind is active in harmonious thoughts or in inharmonious thoughts, whether the mind is strong, firm, and steady, or whether it is weak.

If one continues to think harmonious thoughts it is just like regular beating of the pulse and proper circulation of the blood; if the harmony of thought is broken, then the mind becomes congested. Then a person loses memory; depression comes as the result, and what one sees is nothing but darkness. Doubt, suspicion, distrust, and all manner of distress and despair come when the mind is congested in this way. The Prana of the mind is maintained when the mind can be steady in thoughts of harmony; then the mind can balance its thoughts, then it cannot be easily shaken, then doubt and confusion cannot easily overpower it. Whether it is nervous illness, whether it is mental disorder, whether it is physical illness, at the root of all these different aspects of illness there is one cause, and that cause is inharmony.

The body which has once become inharmonious turns into a receptacle of inharmonious influences, of inharmonious atoms; it partakes of them without knowing it; and so it is with the mind. The body which is already lacking in health is more susceptible to illness than the body which is perfectly healthy; and so the mind which already has a disorder in it is more susceptible to every suggestion of disorder, and in this way goes from bad to worse. Scientists of all ages have found that each element attracts the same element, and so it is natural that illness should attract illness; thus in plain words inharmony attracts inharmony, whereas harmony attracts harmony. We see in everyday life that a person who has nothing the matter with him and is only weak physically, or whose life is not regular, is always susceptible to illness. Then we see that a person who ponders often upon inharmonious thoughts is very easily offended, it does not take long for him to get offended; a little thing here and there makes him feel irritated, because irritation is already there, it wants just a little touch to make it a deeper irritation.

Besides this the harmony of the body and the mind depends upon one's external life, the food one eats, the way one lives, the people one meets, the work one does, the climate in which one lives. There is no doubt that under the same conditions one person may be ill and another may be well. The reason is that one is in harmony with the food he eats, with the weather he lives in, with the people whom he meets, with the conditions around him. Another person revolts against the food he eats, against the people he meets, against the conditions that surround him, against the weather he must live in. This is because he is not in harmony; and he perceives and experiences similar results in all things in his life; disorder and illness are the result.

This idea can be very well demonstrated by the method that

present-day physicians have adopted, of inoculating a person with the same element which makes him ill. There is no better demonstration of this idea than the practice of inoculation. This puts a person in harmony with the thing that is opposed to his nature. If one understands this principle one can inoculate oneself with all that does not agree with one, and with that to which one is continually exposed and from which there is no means of getting away. Woodcutters do not as a rule get sunstroke: seamen do not catch cold easily. The reason is that the former have made themselves sunproof while the latter have made themselves waterproof. In short, the first lesson in health is the understanding of this principle, that illness is nothing but inharmony and that the secret of health lies in harmony.

Disorder of the tone and irregularity in the rhythm are the principal causes of every illness. The explanation of this disorder of the tone is that there is a certain tone which the breath vibrates throughout the body, through every channel of the body; and this tone is a particular tone, continually vibrating, in every person. And when the mystics have said that every person has his note, it is not necessarily the note of the piano, it is the note which is going on as a tone, as a breath. Now, if a person does not take care of himself and allows himself to be influenced by every wind that blows, he, like the water in the sea, goes up and down disturbed by the air. The normal condition is to be able to stand firm through fear, joy, and anxiety; not to let every wind blow one hither and thither like a scrap of paper, but to endure it all and to stand firm and steady through all such influences.

One might say that even water is subject to influences if not the rock. Man is made to be neither rock nor water; he has all in him; he is the fruit of the whole creation, he ought to be able to show his evolution in his balance. A person who is likely to rejoice in a moment and to become depressed in a moment, and who changes his moods, cannot keep that tone which gives him equilibrium and which is the secret of health. How few know that it is not pleasure and merrymaking that give one good health! On the contrary, social life, as it is known today, is merrymaking for one day and afterwards one may be ill for ten days, for that kind of life does not take care of equilibrium. When a person becomes sensitive to every little thing that he comes across, it changes the note of the tone; it becomes a different note to which his body is not accustomed; and that causes an illness. Too much despair or too much joy, everything that is too much should be avoided, although there are natures who always seek extremes; they must have so much joy and amusement that they get tired of it, and then they have a collapse with sorrow and despair. It is among these people that you will find continual illness. If an instrument is not kept in proper tune, if it is knocked about by everyone who comes and handled by everyone, then it gets out of order. The body is an instrument, the most sacred instrument, an instrument which God Himself has made for His divine purpose. If it is kept in tune and the strings are not allowed to become loose, then this instrument becomes the means of that harmony for which God created man.

How must this instrument be kept in tune? In the first place strings of gut and wires of steel both require cleaning. The lungs and veins in the body also require cleaning; it is that which keeps them ready for their work. And how should we clean them? By carefulness in diet, by sobriety, and by breathing properly and correctly; because it is not only water and earth that are used for cleansing, the best means of cleansing is the air and the property that is in the air, the property that we breathe in; and if we knew how by the help of breathing to keep these channels clean, then we should know how to secure health. It is this which maintains the tone, the proper note of each person, without being disturbed. When a person is vibrating his own note which is according to his particular evolution, then he is himself, then he is tuned to the pitch for which he is made, the pitch in which he ought to be and in which he naturally feels comfortable.

And now we come to the rhythm: there is a rhythm of pulsation, the beating of the pulse in the head and in the heart; and whenever the rhythm of this beating is disturbed it causes illness because it disturbs the whole mechanism which is going on, the order of which depends upon the regularity of rhythm. If a person suddenly hears of something causing fear the rhythm is broken, the pulsation changes. Every shock given to a person breaks his rhythm. We very often notice that, however successful an operation, it leaves a mark, even for the rest of one's life. Once the rhythm is broken, it is most difficult to get it right.

If the rhythm has been lost, it must be brought back with great wisdom, because a sudden effort to regain the rhythm may make one lose it still more. If the rhythm has gone too slow or too fast, by trying to bring it to its regular speed one may break the rhythm, and by breaking the rhythm one may break oneself. This should be a gradual process; it must be wisely done. If the rhythm has gone too fast, it must be brought gradually to its proper condition; if it is too slow, it must be gradually made quicker. It requires patience and strength to do it. For instance, someone who tunes the violin wisely does not at once move the peg and bring it to the proper tone, because in the first place it is impossible, and then he always risks breaking the string. However minute may be the difference in the tone, one can bring it to its proper place by gradual tuning; in this way effort is spared and the thing is accomplished.

Gentleness which is taught morally is a different thing, but even gentleness in action and movement is also necessary. In every movement one makes, in every step one takes there must be rhythm. For instance you will find many examples if you look for them of the awkward movements people make; they can never keep well because their rhythm is not right; and that is why illness continues. It may be that no illness can be traced in these people, and yet the very fact of their movements not being in rhythm will keep them out of order. Regularity in habits, in action, in repose, in eating, in drinking, in sitting, in walking, in everything, gives one that rhythm which is necessary and which completes the music of life.

When a child's rhythm and tone are disordered, the healing that a mother can give, often unconsciously, the physicians cannot give in a thousand years. The song she sings, however insignificant, comes from the profound depths of her being and brings with it the healing power. It cures the child in a moment. The caressing, the patting of the mother does more good to the child than any medicine when its rhythm is disturbed and its tone is not good. The mother, even without knowing it distinctly, feels like patting the child when it is out of rhythm, singing to the child when it is out of tune.

And when we come to the mental part of our being, that mechanism is still more delicate than our body. There is a tone also, and every being has a different tone according to his particular evolution, and everyone feels in good health when his own tone is vibrating; but if that tone does not come to its proper pitch, then a person feels lack of comfort, and any illness can arise from it. Every expression of passion, joy, anger, fear, which breaks the continuity of this tone interferes with one's health. Behind the thought there is feeling; and it is the feeling which sustains that tone; the thought is on the surface. In order to keep the continuity of that tone the mystics have special practices.

There used to be a custom in ancient times, that instead of using an organ in churches four or five persons with the lips closed used to keep one tone, humming that one tone together. I was most impressed by this, hearing it again in a church in Russia after coming from India. The secret of the continual ringing of the bell practised by the churches at all times and even up till now, is that it was not only a bell to call people; it was to tune them up to their tone, it was to suggest, 'There is a tone going on in you, get yourself tuned to it!' But if that tuning is not done, even if a person has recovered from his illness, weakness still remains. An external cure is no cure if a person is not cured mentally. If his spirit is not cured the mark of illness remains there and the rhythm of mind is broken.

When a person's mind is going at a speed which is faster or at a speed which is slower than it ought to be, or if a person jumps from one thought to another and so goes on thinking of a thousand things in five minutes, however intellectual he may be, he cannot be normal; or if a person holds one thought and broods on it instead of making progress, he will also cling to his depression, his fears, his disappointments, and that makes him ill. It is irregularity of the rhythm of mind which causes mental disorder.

I do not mean that the rhythm of the mind of one person must be like that of another person. No, each person's rhythm is peculiar to himself. Once a pupil who accompanied me on my walk, in spite of all his kindness and pleasure in accompanying me, felt a great discomfort at times because he could not walk as slowly as I did. Being simple and frank, he expressed this to me. And in answer I said, 'It is a majestic walk.'

The reason was that his rhythm was different. He could not feel comfortable in some other rhythm, he had to be galloping along in order to feel comfortable. And so one can feel what gives one comfort and what gives one discomfort in everything one does. If one does not feel it, that shows that one does not give attention to one's being. The wisdom is to understand oneself. If one can sustain the proper rhythm of one's mind, that is sufficient to keep one healthy.

Mental illnesses are subtler than physical illnesses, though up to now mental illnesses have not been thoroughly explored, but when this has been done we shall find that all physical illnesses have some connection with them. The mind and the body stand face to face. The body reflects its order and disorder upon the mind, the mind reflecting at the same time its harmony and disharmony on the body; and it is for this reason you will find that many who are ill outwardly also have some illness of the mind, and very seldom will one find a case where a person is mentally ill and physically perfectly well.

Once I happened to go to the asylum for the insane in New York, and the physicians very kindly laid before me a number of skulls showing the different cavities in the brain and the spots of decay which had caused insanity in the life of the patients. There is always a sign of it in the physical body. It may be apparent suffering or it may be some decay at the back of it, yet it is not known. I asked them, 'I would like to know whether the cavity brought about the insanity or the insanity brought about the cavity?' Their argument was that the cavity brought about the insanity. But it is not always so, the mental disorder is not always caused by a cavity in the brain; for the inner being has a greater influence on the physical being than the physical body has on the mental existence. Yet it is not always the mind that brings about the physical illness; very often it is so, but not always. Sometimes from the physical plane illness travels to the mental plane, and sometimes illness goes from the mental plane to the physical plane. There are many causes, but in short, if there is a general cause, it is the lack of that music which we call order. Does it not show that man is music, that life is music? In order to play our part best the only thing we can do is to keep our tone and rhythm in proper condition: in this is the fulfilment of our life's purpose.

Movement is life and stillness is death; for in movement there is the significance of life and in stillness we see the sign of death. One might ask if looking at it from a metaphysical point of view there is a stillness. No, but there is what we call no movement, or at least no movement which is perceptible to us in some form, whether it is visible or audible or in the form of sensation or vibration. The movement which is not perceptible to us we name stillness; the word life we use only in connection with the perceptible existence, the movement of which we perceive. Therefore, with regard to our physical health, movement is the principal thing, regulation of movement, of its rhythm in pulsation and the circulation of the blood. The whole cause of death and decay is to be traced to the lack of movement; all different aspects of diseases are to be traced to congestion. Every decay is caused by congestion, and congestion is caused by lack of movement. There are parts of the body where the veins, the nerves, adhere to the skin and there is no free circulation. There arise all sorts of diseases. Outer diseases of that kind we call skin diseases; when it works inwardly it manifests in the form of a certain pain. A physician may show us a thousand different reasons as being the cause of different diseases, but the one and central cause of each disease and of all diseases is lack of movement, which is in fact lack of life. This mechanism of the body is made to work according to a certain rhythm, and is maintained by a perpetual rhythmic movement. The centre of that perpetual current of life is the breath. The different remedies that man has found in all ages often bring cure to sufferers for a time, but they are not always completely cured, for the cause of the disease remains unexplored. At the back of all illness the cause is some irregular, unnatural living in the way of food or drink or action or repose.

Death is a change that comes through the inability of the body to hold what we call the soul. The body has a certain amount of magnetism, which is the sign of its perfect running order. When, owing to illness, the body, either suddenly or gradually, loses that magnetism by the power of which it holds the soul, it so to speak helplessly loses its grip upon something that it was holding; and it is this losing of the grip that is known to us as death. Generally it is a gradual process. A little pain, a little illness, a little discomfort first manifest themselves. One does not take notice of it, but in time it grows into an illness.

Very often diseases are maintained by the patients' not knowing that they are maintaining them, just by their ignorance of their condition, by their neglect of themselves. There is a larger number of patients who leave their condition to be studied by the doctor. They do not know what is the matter with them, from the beginning to the end of the illness. As in ancient times simple believers trusted the priest to send them to heaven or to the other place, so today the patient gives himself into the hands of the doctor. Can anyone with keen observation imagine that anybody else is capable of knowing as much about oneself as one could know oneself if one wished to?

Is it a fault not to wish this? No, it is a habit. It is a kind of neglect of oneself that one does not think about one's condition oneself and wants the physician to tell one what is the matter. The pain is in oneself, one can be the best judge of one's life; one can find out the cause behind one's own illness, because one knows one's life best. Numberless souls today living this way, ignorant of their own condition, depend upon someone who has studied medical science outwardly. Even the physician cannot help one properly if one does not know one's condition clearly. It is one's own clear knowledge of one's complaint that enables one to give the physician a correct idea. When there is a little hole in the cloth, if one does not look to it it will tear easily and become a large hole. So it is with health. If there is something a little wrong with it, one neglects it, absorbed in life as it is, and so allows it to become worse every day, drawing closer thereby the death which otherwise could have been avoided.

The question is, if it is right that one should think of one's body and the condition of one's health. It is, so long as one is not obsessed by oneself. If one thinks about one's health so much that one becomes obsessed by it, it is working against oneself. It is certainly wrong, because it is not helping oneself. If one pities oneself and says, 'Oh, how ill I am, and how terrible it is! And shall I ever be well?' then the impression becomes a kind of fuel to the fire, one is feeding one's illness by the thought of it. But if on the other hand one becomes so neglectful of oneself that one says, 'Oh, it does not matter; it is after all an illusion,' one will not be able to keep that thought when the pain increases. It is as necessary to take care of oneself as it is to forget about one's illness. For an illness comes to a person as a thief enters the house, quietly. He works without the knowledge of the dwellers in it and robs them of their best treasures. If one keeps guard against it, it is not wrong as long as one does not dwell all the time on one's illness.

One might ask, 'Is it worth while to be alive? Why must we not end this life? What is it, after all?' But this is an abnormal thought. A person with a normal body and mind will not think in this way. When this abnormal thought grows it culminates in insanity, which causes many people to commit suicide. The natural desire of every soul is to live, to have a life of perfect health, to make the best of one's coming into this world. Neither

God nor the soul is pleased with the desire for death, for death does not belong to the soul. It is a kind of agitation, a revolt that arises in the mind of someone, who then says, 'I prefer death to life.' To have the desire to live, and yet to live a life of suffering is also not a wise thing. And if wisdom counts for anything, one must spare no effort to arrive at the proper condition of health.

In ancient times people attributed the cause of every illness to spirits. There was a spirit of every kind of illness, and they believed that particular spirit brought that illness. The healers made attempts to cure every patient that came with that illness, and they were successful in making them well. Today that spirit of illness has caused a material manifestation, for the physicians now declare that at the root of every illness is a germ, a microbe. Every day a new invention brings a new microbe to their eyes. And if a new microbe is discovered every day till the end of the world numberless microbes will be discovered and there will be numberless diseases; in the end it will be difficult to find one man healthy, for there must always be some microbe; if it is not of an old disease, then of a newly discovered one. As this is a world of innumerable lives, it will always show innumerable lives; each life having its power, constructive or destructive, will show that power even in a microbe; and so this discovery of microbes of diseases will go on with the increase of diseases, for to prevent microbes from existing is not always in the power of man. Sometimes he will destroy them, but often he will find that each microbe destroyed will produce in return many more microbes. What is life? Every atom of it is living, call it ray or electron, germ or microbe.

The people of old thought that they were spirits, living beings,

in the absence of science which today distinguishes these spirits in the form of microbes; and yet it seems that the ancient healers had a greater grip upon the illness, for the reason that they did not see the outer microbe only, but the microbe in its spirit. In destroying the microbe they did not only destroy the outer microbe, but the inner microbe in the form of the spirit, of the germ; and the most interesting thing is that in order to drive away that spirit which they thought had possessed the patient, they burned or they placed before him certain chemicals which are used even now, having been proved to be destructive to the germs of diseases.

With every measure that physicians may take to prevent the germs of diseases from coming, in spite of all the success that they will have there will be a greater failure; for even if the actual germ is destroyed, it exists, its family exists, somewhere. Besides, the body which has once become the abode of that particular germ has become a receptacle of the same germ. If the physician destroys the germ of disease from the body of an individual, that does not mean that he destroys it from the universe. This problem, therefore, must be looked at from another point of view: that everything that exists in the objective world has its living and more important part existing in the subjective world; and that part which is in the subjective is held by the belief of the patient. As long as the patient believes that he is ill he is giving sustenance to that part of the disease which is in the subjective world. Even if the germs of the disease were destroyed, not once but a thousand times in his body, they would be created there again; because the source from which the germs spring is in his belief, not in his body, as the source of the whole creation is within, not without.

The outer treatment of many such diseases is just like cutting the plant from its stem while the root remains in the ground. Since the root of the illness is in the subjective part of one's being, in order to drive away that illness one must dig out the root by taking away the belief of illness even before the outer germ is destroyed. The germ of illness cannot exist without the force, the breath, which it receives from the subjective part of one's being; and if the source of its sustenance is once destroyed, then the cure is certain.

Very few people can hold a thought, but many are held by a thought. If such a simple thing as holding a thought were mastered, the whole life would be mastered. When once a person gets into his head, 'I am ill', and when this is confirmed by a physician, then his belief becomes watered like a plant, then his continual reflection of it, falling upon his illness like the sun, makes the plant of illness grow; and therefore it would not be an exaggeration to say that, consciously or unconsciously, the patient is the gardener of his own illness.

One might ask, 'Is it, then, right not to trouble about microbes? If a physician finds them and shows them to us, should we not believe it?' You cannot help believing it if you have gone so far as to make the physician show it to you. You have helped the physician to believe it, and now you are wondering whether you should believe it yourself. You cannot help believing something which has been shown to you, which is before you. No doubt if you rise above this, then you have touched the truth; for when you rise above facts you touch reality. Is it not deluding oneself to deny facts? It is no more deluding than one is already deluded. Facts themselves are delusions; it is the rising above this delusion that enables one to touch reality. As long as the brain is muddled with facts, it will be increasingly absorbed every day in the puzzle of life, making life more confused than ever before. It is because of this that the Master taught, 'Seek ye first the Kingdom of God.' This means: 'Rise above facts first, and by the light that you gain from there, thrown upon facts, you will see the facts in a clear light.'

This does not mean at all that you should close your eyes to facts. It only means, 'Look up first and when your eyes are once charged with divine light, then when you cast your glance on the world of facts you will have a much clearer vision, the vision of reality.' There is no lack of honesty if you deny the fact of illness; it is no hypocrisy if you deny it to yourself first. It is only a help, for there are many things in life that exist because they are sustained by your acknowledging their existence. Deluded by outwardly appearing facts you hold them in your thought as a belief; but by denying them you root them out, for they cannot exist when starved of the sustenance for which they depend upon you.

❧

This does not mean that the fact of germs should altogether be ignored, for it is not possible to ignore something which you see; besides it does not mean that the discovery of microbes has not been of use to the physicians, enabling them to attend better to the patient. Yet at the same time one can be too sensitive to germs, one can exaggerate the idea of germs, making the idea more than the reality. But one person will be susceptible to those germs and tend to be their victim; while another person assimilates those germs and thus destroys them. In other words, the one is destroyed by germs and the other destroys them. It is said that contagious diseases are contracted by the microbes going from one person to another, in the breath, in the air, in everything; but it is not always the microbes, it is very often the impression. When a person has seen that his friend has caught a cold and has thought, 'I fear I shall catch it,' he has certainly caught the disease; because he has been afraid and has been impressed by it, he has caught it. It is not always necessary that the germs of the cold should have gone from one person to another by way of the breath; the impression that a person has received can create them, for behind the whole of creation there is that power. We often see that the more a person is afraid of a thing, the more he is pursued by it, for unconsciously he concentrates upon it.

There are germs and impurities, but there are also elements to purify them. Those five elements, earth, water, fire, air, and ether, as spoken of by the mystics, do not only compose germs, but can also destroy them, if one only knew how one could make use of those five elements to purify one's body with them and also one's mind. As there is need of sun and water for plants to grow, so there is need of the five elements for a person to keep in perfect health. These five elements he breathes according to his capacity of breath. But by breath every person does not attract the same properties; for everyone attracts from the breath elements according to his particular constitution. One attracts more fire element in his breath, another more water element, and a third attracts more earth element. Sometimes one receives an element which one does not require. Besides, the sun currents have a greater healing power than anything else. A person who knows how to breathe perfectly, who is attracting sun currents into his body, can keep the body free from every kind of impurity. No microbes of destruction can exist if the sun currents can touch every part of the body which is within, and that is done by the breath. The places of the earth which are hidden from the sun, which are not touched by the air, become damp; several little lives are created there, germs of destruction are born, and the air in that place becomes dense. If this is true, then the body also needs the sun and air. The lungs, intestines, and veins and tubes of the body all need the sun and the air; and these are taken in by means of perfect breathing; and even the mind derives benefit from this. For the mind too is composed of five elements, the elements in their finer condition.

Rest and repose as well as action and movement must have a certain balance, a certain rhythm. If there is no balance between activity and repose, then the breath is not secure either. Our great mistake is that with every little complaint the first thing we think of is the doctor. We never stop to think, 'What has been the cause in myself? Have I been too active, too lazy? Have I not been careful about my diet, about my sleep? Have I not breathed in all the elements which are necessary to keep this mechanism of body and mind going?' Frightened by every illness, a man first runs to the doctor. As long as the illness has not appeared before him he does not mind if it is growing inwardly without his having noticed it. It may continue to grow for a long time; for years the man, absorbed in his outer activities, never thinks that he is giving a home to his worst enemy in his body. Thus very often illness is caused by negligence.

Then there are others who become too careful, they think of nothing else except their illness. The first question before them is, 'How shall I get well?' Pondering upon their illness they give a kind of fuel to that fire of illness from their thoughts, keeping it burning; they do not know that by their unconscious effort the illness is kept alive. In order to keep the health in perfect order one must keep a balance between body and mind, between activity and repose; and it is the psychological outlook on one's health which helps more than any medicines.

I remember going to see a patient who had been suffering from an illness for more than twenty years and had lost every hope of getting better. Several physicians had been consulted, many different treatments had been tried. I told her a simple thing to do; I did not teach any special practices, but just an ordinary little thing to do in the morning and in the evening; and to the great surprise of those at home, she began to move her hands and legs, which had been thought impossible; and this gave them great hope, that a patient who had been so long in bed could do this, and to her too it was a great surprise. I went to see them after a few days and asked them, 'How is the patient progressing?' They said, 'She is progressing very well. We could never have believed that she could move her hands and legs; it is the most wonderful thing. But we cannot make her believe that now after twenty years of suffering she can ever be well again. This illness has made such an impression upon her that she thinks that it is natural for her, and that to be well is a dream, an unreality.'

This gave me the idea that when a person lives in a certain condition for a long, long time, that condition becomes his friend unconsciously. He does not know it, he may think that he wants to get out of it, yet there is some part of his being that is holding his illness just the same.

One day, remembering this peculiarity of human nature, I asked someone who was brought to me to be cured of an obsession how long she had had this obsession. She explained to me how horrible the obsession was, how terrible life was for her. I listened to it for half an hour, everything that she said against the obsession; but recollecting this amusing aspect of human nature, I asked her, 'You do not really mean to say that you want to get rid of that spirit? If I had this spirit I would keep it. After all these years that you have had it, it seems unjust and very cruel to this spirit. If this spirit had not cared for you, it would not have stayed with you all these years. In this world, is it easy for a person to remain so long with one? This spirit is most faithful.' Then she said, 'I do not really want to get rid of it.' I was very much amused to see how this person wanted sympathy and help, but did not want to give up the spirit. It was not the spirit that was obsessing this person, but the person was obsessing the spirit!

Psychic natures are more liable to illness, as they are more susceptible to gross vibrations, and especially those inclined to spiritualistic seances. Their bodies become so susceptible to any kind of illness, also to obsessions, that in reality they prepare themselves to welcome in their own spirit any other spirit.

◦◦

As medical science has advanced in modern times the different diseases and complaints have become more classified. Each separate complaint has been given a certain name, and in this way even if a person has only a slight complaint, after the examination by a physician he is told its name. His complaint may be only as big as a molehill, but it is turned into a mountain. There is no greater misfortune than hearing from a doctor that one has contracted an illness which is dangerous, the name of which is frightening. What then happens? That name being impressed on the heart of the man, creates the same element and in the end the man sees the thing come true about which he was told by the physician. In the same way the impression that the words of a fortune-teller make upon one in many cases brings about the realization of his fortune-telling in the end. The fortune-teller is not always a saint, he is not always a clairvoyant who sees what he claims to see; he may be only an imaginative person. But he has said something and that impression has remained with the person; and in the end he realizes that it came true. Then what an impression a physician makes who is authorized by the medical authorities, in whom one immediately places one's trust, even if he was mistaken in finding the real disease; because among a hundred physicians there is hardly one who has insight into the real nature and character of a disease, and among a hundred patients the physician can perhaps only tell correctly the nature and character of one man's complaint. Thus there is great danger of a person being impressed at the beginning of his illness by a right or wrong remark made by a physician about that illness. Among ancient peoples only the physicians knew the names of diseases; but the physician was not allowed to tell the patient what complaint he had, because from a psychological point of view he would be doing wrong. This was not only a medical science, there was a psychological idea attached to it.

I have seen numberless cases come to me frightened by something that a physician had said to them. Perhaps there is nothing the matter with them, or only a little illness; perhaps they have not yet realized what it is, but they are frightened just the same. And if there is an imaginative patient, then he has a wide scope for his imagination. Everything that is wrong, he attaches to something he has heard from the physician, he relates every condition of his life to that particular remark. In life such as we live it in the world, with so many things to do, so many responsibilities resting upon us at home and in the outside world, and with the strife that is reflected upon us by our life in this world, we naturally have our ups and downs physically. Sometimes one is tired; sometimes one needs a rest; sometimes one must fast one day, one day there is no inclination for food. If one attributes all these little things to an illness that a physician has once told of, one is certainly making the illness strong; for the root of illness is in the mind, and if that root is watered all the time by thought and feeling, then illness is realized in the end.

When we look at the surgical world, no doubt wonderful operations are being done, and humanity has experienced great help through surgical operations; yet it is still experimental, and it will take perhaps a century longer for surgery to mature. It is in its infancy just now. The first impulse of a surgeon is to look at a case only from one point of view, and to think that this case can be cured by surgery. He has no other thought in his mind, he has no time to think that there is another possibility. If he is a wise surgeon, he gives a word of confidence; yet he knows that it is an experiment. It is a person he is dealing with, and not a piece of wood or a stone that can be carved and engraved upon. It is a person with feeling, it is a soul which is experiencing life through every atom that it has, a soul which is not made for a knife. Now this person has to go through this experience, fearing death, preferring life to death. Very often what happens is that what was considered wrong before the operation, is found to have been right afterwards. No doubt something wrong has to be produced because the operation has been performed. And an operation is not something that is finished; it is something which has its action upon the nerves and then upon the spirit of a man, and then its reaction upon life again. Do we not see that after an operation a person's whole life has become impressed with it? A certain strain on the nerves, a certain upset in the spirit has been caused. The care of the surgeon continues only until the patient is apparently well, outwardly well; but what about the after-effect of it on the spirit of the person, on his mind, its reaction on his life? The surgeon does not always realize this, he is not concerned with it.

Cure means absolute cure, within and without. By this it is not meant that surgery has no place in the scheme of life. It is a most important part of the medical world, but at the same time it must be avoided when it can be avoided; one must not lightly jump into it. A young person with strength and energy thinks, 'What is it? I can go through it.' But once done, there remains an impression for the whole life. Man has intuition as his heritage, and it is intuition which is the basis of every science. At this time when science is treated as a book study, it takes away the part that intuition must perform. If in the medical world an intuitive development were introduced, if many physicians were occupied in finding remedies by which to avoid operations, surely a very great work could be accomplished. It is amusing that at one time when the operation for appendicitis began to be known in the United States, it became a fashion among the rich people to have that operation done because a few days at home are quite pleasant. And then the physicians began to choose appendicitis patients among those who had the means to stay at home for some time and rest. Everybody asked, 'Did you have it?' 'Yes, I had it.' It was just like a game.

Another subject is the use of drugs. Any physician, after life-long experience, will find that often he has prescribed drugs for people, and although he may have seemed to cure them for the time being, yet he was not really successful. The after-effects of drugs are sometimes so depleting, and the confusion that they create in the brain and mind so great, that they can ruin a person's life. I have seen many people who, after medical treatment for their illness, once accustomed to drugs, have made their body a kind of receptacle for drugs. They live upon the drug and cannot live without it. In order to digest their food they must have something, in order to sleep they must have something, in order to feel cheerful they must have some drug. Now, when these natural things such as digesting one's food, being gay and cheerful, sleeping comfortably, which are natural blessings, depend upon outside, material things, how can that person be called healthy? In order to make the best of today they take a drug, and then tomorrow becomes worse.

When we consider that the human body is an instrument that God created for His own experience, then what a mistake it must be to allow this body, through drugs and medicines, to become unfit for the use of the divine Spirit. It is not meant by this that medicine is never necessary. Medicine has its place; even drugs, when there is that necessity. But when a drug is used for little things that can be cured by some other means, in the end the health gets out of hand and even drugs cannot give the person rest. The best medicine is a pure diet, nourishing food, fresh air, regularity in action and repose, clearness of thought, pureness

of feeling, and confidence in the perfect Being, with whom we are linked and whose expression we are. That is the essence of health. The more we realize this, the more secure will be our health.

I knew a person whom a physician had examined and had told that he would die within three months, No doubt if that person had been imaginative he would have taken that impression. But he came to me and he said, 'What nonsense! Die in three months! I am not going to die even in three hundred years from now.' And to our great surprise within three months the doctor died and this man brought me the news! We must learn to respect the human being and realize that a human soul is beyond birth and death, that a human soul has a divine spirit in it, and that all illnesses and pains and sufferings are only his tests and trials. He is above them, and we must try to raise him above illnesses.

Behind everything there is movement, vibration. What causes a certain movement of particles of matter is vibration. Vibration is felt by us, it is realized by our senses as a certain movement of particles of matter, but vibration in itself is a movement. It is because of this that the power of the word is stronger than any medicine or any other treatment or operation, because the word causes certain vibrations in our body, in the atmosphere, in our environment, bringing about thereby a cure which nothing else can bring about. When we see a healthy person and a person suffering from some illness, and we think of the condition of their pulsation and of the circulation of their blood, we shall find that behind it all there is a movement, there is a vibration which is going on. In one person that vibration is in a proper condition, there is health; in the other person vibration is not in its right condition, therefore there is illness.

There was a physician in America who happened to think of this. Only, the difference is that when a scientist thinks of such a thing, even if it comes by intuition, he pursues it by going from the foot of the mountain towards the top. And it is very difficult to climb the mountain, and very often before he has climbed the mountain his life is ended. The physician is now dead. His was a very good idea. Although he had not come to the secret of it, yet as an idea it inspired many physicians in the United States and in the world, and it created great excitement in the medical world. But, as the mystics say, seek ye first the Kingdom of God . . . and all these things shall be added unto you. That is another way. That is not climbing from the bottom to the top, which is so difficult; it is climbing; it is first reaching the top, and then all is easy. It is easy for the one who is on the top of the mountain to move anywhere he likes from the top. It does not take so much energy, it does not weigh him down. Avicenna, the great physician of ancient times, on whose discoveries medieval science was based, was a Sufi who used to sit in meditation, and by intuition he used to write prescriptions. Just lately a physician has discovered the great treasure that this man had given to medical science and has written a book to interpret the ideas of Avicenna in modern language.

⁓◦⊗◦⁓

Most of the cases of physical and mental illness come from exhaustion of the nerves. Not everybody knows to what extent to use nerve force in everyday life and to what extent to control it. Very often a good person, a kind, loving, affectionate person, gives out his energy at every call from every side, and so, continually giving energy, in the end finds his nerves troubled and weakened. In the end the same person who was once kind and nice and polite cannot keep this up, because when the funds of energy have expired, then there is no control, there is no power of endurance, there is no patience to take things easily.

Then the person who once proved to be good and kind becomes irritable and troubled, and tired and disgusted with things. Very often it may be called abuse of goodness; for it is not always giving out that answers the demands of everyday life; it is the balanced condition of one's body and mind which answers the demands of life satisfactorily. And sometimes it becomes a passion with a person to waste his energy either in doing something or in speaking continually; and this passion can grow to such an extent that even when that person has lost a great deal of his energy, he will still find satisfaction in giving out even more. In the presence of that person others will feel depleted, because he has no energy left, he is trying to give out what little he has, and the irritation and strain fall upon the others; it makes them nervous also.

Weakness of nerves is not only the cause of physical diseases, but it leads to insanity. There is one principal cause of physical diseases as well as of mental diseases: overstrained nerves, exhausted nerves; and that person whose nerves are exhausted, in spite of all virtue and goodness, goodwill and desire to do right, will prove to be doing wrong, to his own surprise, because he has lost self-discipline. His high ideals are of no use to him, for he has not got himself in hand. His qualifications, his knowledge, his attitude, his morals will all prove to be futile in the absence of that nervous force which keeps man fit and capable of doing all that it is proper for him to do in the world.

Lack of soberness also causes nervous exhaustion. Therefore all alcoholic and intoxicating things consume the energy of the nerves, eat the energy of the nerves. One might ask why a person takes delight in such things, and again the answer is that it is a passion; that anything that produces intoxication for the moment, that excites the nerves, makes one feel, so to speak, more cheerful for that moment. But one depends upon something outside, and the reaction comes when the effect of that intoxicant has worn off. Then one feels twice as weak and exhausted as before, and needs twice the amount of drug or alcohol in order to make one feel, for a few hours, as cheerful as one did. And so one goes on and on until one has no power over mind and body but becomes a slave to something one takes. That is the only time that such a person thinks he lives; at all other times he feels miserable. That becomes his world, his heaven, his paradise, his life. All manner of excess in passion and anger, all manner of sensual life and rejoicing in it robs one of the energy, the power and vitality of the nerves.

Besides, every effect that is created in voice, in word, in singing, is created by the nervous power; the whole secret of magnetism is in the nerves. The whole secret of success of a public man, a public person on the stage or in the concert-hall is his nervous power, the success of the lawyer, of the barrister in the court is his nervous power. It will always be found that a good barrister who has made a name has that power, and it is magnetism. Therefore the sign of a person with health, both physical and mental, is that he develops that influence which is expressed by nervous power, and it has its influence upon all things.

Strength gives one more power, weakness causes a greater weakness. The proper condition of the nerves enables one to impress. A person nervously depleted, even if he be in the right, cannot impress it upon another, because there is no strength behind it. And so even if he is in the right, he will be at a loss what to do. There is no power to go forward, to stand up for his own right.

The system that we know today of keeping patients shut up in hospitals, in asylums, is just like making them captives to the disease. The atmosphere of the place and the very thought of being in the hospital make them feel ill; and so it is with the life in asylums. However efficient the treatment may be, it gives a person the impression that he is out of his mind, there is something wrong with his mind; and the whole atmosphere suggests the same thing. Besides, it would be kinder on the part of society and of the family, if the patients could be taken in hand by friends or relations in their difficult times. They could be helped better than by putting them in places where they can think of nothing but their illness. I have myself seen many cases whom relations or friends have looked after, and they have been helped much more than by what they would have received in a hospital.

One might say that medical treatments require a special place for such things, and that there they have everything besides the physician to look after them, and that that is the only way in large cities that such cases can be looked after. Yes, it is true, and one cannot help it where the situation is difficult; still, where it can be helped one should try to help.

Nervous diseases are very often treated by giving medicines. There is no medicine in the world which can do good to nerves; for nerves are the most natural part of one's being. They are the part of one's being which is linked with the physical world and with the mental world, it is the central part of one's being; and there is no better remedy for nerves than nature, a life of rest and repose, quiet, proper breathing, proper nourishment, and someone to treat the patient with wisdom. By understanding the law of environment and climatic influences, by understanding what influences people have upon such a patient, one can cure him.

Nervous energy is a kind of battery for the whole mechanism of the mind and body. For the mechanism of mind, therefore, it is the clearness of the nervous mechanism and the good working of the nervous mechanism which enable us to make our thought clear to ourselves, or to hold our thought, or to imagine, or to think, or to memorize; and when the nervous system is not clear, then one cannot keep things in mind, conceive things in the mind, or keep to one thought, and various conditions of mental disorder begin to show. Within the body the nervous system is called centres by Yogis. The different centres are the points of the nervous system, the centres through which one experiences intuition, one feels, one observes keenly.

And now the question is where to get nervous energy, and how to get it. Our body and mind are a battery of that power, they are made of it, we are that power. The magnetism of a human being is much greater than anything else in the world. No jewel, no gem, no flower, no fruit, nothing in the world has such magic as a human being has if he knows how to retain it, how to keep himself in that condition. Because with all the scientific discoveries of radium and electrons and all the different atoms, there is no atom in the world which is more radiant than the atoms with which the human body is composed, atoms which are not only attractive to the human eye, but attract the whole of creation towards the human being. The horse serves man, the camel carries his load, the tiger surrenders to man, the elephants walk by his command. But when he loses his proper spirit, then it is just like losing salt: as it is said in the Bible, 'Ye are the salt of the earth, and when the salt hath lost its savour, wherewith shall it be salted?' When man's own body, his own spirit, are more radiant than anything else, then there is nothing else that can give him more spirit. He himself is the spirit.

⟨∞⟩

One often wonders to what extent the spirit has power over matter; and the answer is that, as matter is the outcome of spirit, spirit has all power over matter. One becomes pessimistic after having tried the power of thought to cure oneself or to cure others, and failed; and then one begins to think that it is not the spirit that can help, it is something outside. It is not meant for one moment that the things outside have no effect, but that the spirit has all power to cure a person of every malady. No doubt in order to cure every malady the spirit must reach a state so high that it is able to do so perfectly. In the present age a person thinks that spirit is born of matter. Through biological study one begins to realize that first there was matter, and then it evolved, until in man it developed and sprang up as an intelligence, as a human intelligence; but according to the mystic the whole thing is a play of the intelligence. In the rock, in the tree, in the plant, in the animal, and in man the intelligence has gone all along and developed itself, and through man it comes to its pure essence. And it is arriving at the pure essence that makes man become aware of his origin.

Christian Science teaches that matter does not exist. Even if it does not explain it fully, nevertheless there is one life; and what we call matter and spirit are simply different aspects of it. We must realize that there is one life and that it is all spirit; even matter is a passing state of spirit. And spirit is intelligent; it is intelligence itself, besides being powerful and free from death and decay. It is capable of giving its life even to the dense substance which has been made out of itself, and which is matter. Therefore it is beyond words to tell to what an extent the thought, the feeling, and the attitude help one to become cured.

The feeling that through the nerve-channels, through the veins and tubes, it is the divine blood that is circulating, which is perfect, which is complete, which is pure, helps one very much. In other words, what is illness? Illness is an inharmony. If inharmony causes illness and failure, so harmony brings the cure. If one can harmonize one's life in every way, in every form, certainly it must result in a perfect harmony, and that will manifest also as the cure of illness. No doubt sorrow can cause all illnesses, because it makes both mind and body inharmonious, and then one can easily catch an illness. To me a really brave person is he who says, 'What has happened has happened; what I am going through I shall rise above; and what will come I shall meet with courage.' If one wants to be sad, there are many things that can make one sad. One need not wait for causes to arise that make one shed tears; every moment one could shed tears if one had that inclination. One should not look for ill-luck. Ill-luck can easily be found everywhere if one will look for it; and many unconsciously do so. There are many illnesses, but hopelessness is the worst illness. When a person has lost hope his illness cannot be cured. Hope is part of intelligence, hope is the strength of intelligence. If intelligence works against all disorder, whether physical or mental or moral disorder, certainly a cure can be obtained.

The mystics have always known and practised in a most perfect way the idea which is generally talked about in its most elementary form—the idea that by repeating to oneself, 'I am well, I am better, I am better,' one becomes better. There are many who do not see any reason in it, but you will see that in time the most materialistic people will come to realize the truth that it is the attitude of mind, the willingness to be cured, the desire to get above one's illness, the inclination to fight against disorder, which help one to health.

There is a difference between belief and thought. One might say, 'I am thinking every day I shall get well, but that does not come to pass.' Yes, thought is one thing, belief is another. When you compare thought with belief, one is automatic, the other is more living. And when a person says, 'I am thinking, or, I am practising this every day, but I don't get any benefit', it only means that he is practising one thing and believing another. He is practising, 'I shall be well', and he is believing, 'I am ill'. It may be his unconscious belief, but there is a belief: 'This will not cure me, I shall continue to be ill'; and though he may be repeating a thousand times a day, 'I shall be well, I shall be well',

When a child is ill it can be helped by helpful thought. Sometimes the mother's healing thought, the mother's sympathy, works with the child more successfully than any medicine that is given to the child; and in this is the proof of the power of healing. There are numberless cases that can be observed when consciously, or even unconsciously, the desire of the mother for the child to recover becomes a healing influence. If a mother is anxious and worries about a child, no doubt that has a contrary effect; because unconsciously the mother then holds an illness in her thought for the child.

The way that mystical healers have brought about wonderful cures is beyond comprehension. What thought-power can do is seen in their work. No doubt if a person is a hindrance to healing influences, then even a healer cannot do his work properly; but if a person's attitude is right, if one believes that spirit has all the power to cure, certainly one can be cured. The mystics have proved in their lives that not only their power can cure, but even death stands before them as their obedient servant. Death for them is not a constable who arrests and takes a person when the time has come, death for them is a porter that carries their baggage when travelling. But healing apart, even medicine will not do any good to a pessimistic person. If he does not believe in it, it has no power over him.

If belief makes even the power of medicine perfect, then how much more can it do if one believes in the power of the spirit over matter. What generally happens is that one does not know if there is a spirit. Often one wonders if there is any spirit, for what one knows is matter. Once, when travelling on a ship, a young Italian came to me and said, 'I only believe in eternal matter.' I said, 'Your belief is not very different from my belief.' He was very surprised to hear a priest (he thought that I was a priest) saying such a thing. He asked, 'What is your belief?' I said, 'What you call eternal matter, I call eternal spirit. You call matter what I call spirit. What does it signify? It is only a difference in words. It is one Eternal.' He became very interested from that time; before that he was very much afraid.

The secret of healing is to rise by the power of belief above the limitations of this world of variety, that one may touch by the power of intelligence the oneness of the whole Being. It is there that one becomes charged with the almighty power, and it is by the power of that attainment that one is able to help oneself and others in their pain and suffering. Verily, spirit has all the power there is.

～◦∞◦～

The idea of calling certain diseases incurable is the great mistake that man makes today. It is really that he has not got the remedy for curing those diseases, and so he calls them incurable. But by calling a certain disease incurable he makes that patient hopeless, not only regarding the help of man, but also regarding the help that he can get from above; therefore it cannot be a right idea to make a living being believe that there is no cure for him. If the source and goal are perfect, then the attainment of perfection is possible; and as health is a perfection, it can be attained. All the strength is in the spirit. Everyone has strength to the extent that he is close to the spirit, but everyone has a spark of that spirit in himself; and everyone should know that he has a responsibility for his own health as a healer to himself, and that he has a part to play for himself that is not only a physician's responsibility or a healer's. But at the same time he must be ready first to play his part as a physician, as a healer, himself; first to see what is his condition, what is lacking, what is the matter with him, how to heal. If he cannot do it well enough he may ask another to help him, but he must be the first to desire it.

Is healing by hypnotism a desirable method? Now surgeons make use of ether in order to perform operations. Although it is harmful to the patient, yet at the same time it is necessary; and so if this way is used to make a person better, if it is necessary, it may be allowed. Every person, however, should be able to care for himself by prayer, by meditation, by silence, and to cherish that belief in perfect health and root out the belief in illness.

Curing by magnetism is another thing. It is another form of prescription. There is a prescription given by a physician, a certain medicine is given to act or to react against a certain condition. So the power which is the life-energy is given in a certain form in order to give the patient what he lacks. It is not exactly an objective remedy, but it is external just the same.

There is no illness which is incurable; and we commit a sin against the perfection of the divine Being when we give up hope of any person's cure, for in that perfection nothing is impossible; all is possible. We see it with our limited reason, and make the divine perfection small, as small as we are; but in reality the vastness, the greatness of the almighty power is beyond our comprehension, and limiting it would be nothing but an error. What generally happens in the case of what is called incurable disease is that the impression made upon the patient of knowing and feeling that his disease cannot be cured becomes the root of his illness, and so the illness becomes rooted in the belief of the patient. Then no remedy, no help can root it out. The best treatment that a healer, a physician, can give to a patient is to give him first the belief that he can be cured, then medicine or healing treatment, whatever method he may adopt to cure him.

We hear accounts of the physicians of ancient times, of the mystics and thinkers, that they used to find out a person's illness just by looking at him. This came by intuition; and if the people in past ages were proficient in it, it does not mean that the soul has lost this quality. Even today, if one develops that quality one can find out at the first glance all that is wrong with a person in body, mind, and spirit—all. For his outward expression tells of the inner condition; any disorder in the spirit, mind, or body is clearly manifested outwardly; and it is only a matter of developing that faculty in order to read it and to find it out. When this faculty is developed a little further it makes one know also what is the reason behind every illness that a person has, whether mental or physical; and when this faculty is developed still further, one can also find out what would be the best way, the best remedy to cure this person. Avicenna, the great mystic of Persia, was a physician and a healer at the same time. The mystic is a healer by nature, but the attainment of the outer knowledge enables him to use his faculty best in the work of healing.

What must one do in order to develop this faculty, to find out if one has this faculty in oneself? As a mechanism wants winding every day, or a musical instrument wants tuning, so every person, whatever be his life and occupation, wants tuning every day. And what is this tuning? This tuning is the harmonizing of every action of the mechanism of the body, the harmonizing of the pulsation, of the beating of the head and heart, of the circulation of the blood; and this can be done by the proper method of repose. When once this is done, then the next step is to harmonize the condition of the mind. The mind which is constantly wandering, which is not under the control of the will, which cannot be made to respond in a moment, which is restless, this mind should be harmonized; it can be harmonized first with the will. When there is harmony between the will and the mind, then the body and mind, thus controlled and harmonized, become one harmonious mechanism working automatically. Merely bringing the mind and body into order allows one's every faculty to show itself in its fullness, to manifest. A person begins to observe life more keenly, to comprehend life more fully; and so perception becomes keener and the faculty of knowing develops.

No doubt the more a person evolves, the more he gains insight into the lives of things and beings. The first thing is to understand the condition of one's own body, the physical health, the mental condition; and when one can understand one's own condition better, then to begin to see the condition of another person. Then intuition is born and becomes active. As a man develops intuitively he begins to see the pains and sufferings of people; and if this sympathy grows and becomes vaster, his sight becomes more keen and he begins to observe the reason behind the complaint; and if he goes still further in the path of intuition, he begins also to see what remedy would be the best one for the person who suffers.

Furthermore, there are some signs a seer sees, outward signs which explain the fundamental principles of health. Every person represents the sun, his heart, his spirit, his body, all of him; and there is, as in the case of the sun, the sunrise and the sunset. There is a tendency of the body which draws it towards the earth, which shows the sunset, because the soul is drawing itself towards the goal. And there is another tendency which is like the sunrise, and that is that the body is naturally inclined to raise itself. It seems that the earth is not drawing the body, it is something above which draws it; that is the sign of the sunrise. And it does not depend upon the age, it depends upon the condition of the harmony that is established between the spirit and the body. For a mystic it is quite usual to know if a person is going to die in three years' time, and easier still to know if a person is to die in a year. Apart from the inner spirit, even the tendency, the inclination of the body gives every sign.

～⟨∞⟩～

There are different ways of looking at illness. One person will look at an illness as a punishment from above; another person looks at it as a punishment brought about by his own misdeeds; there is another way of looking at illness, and that is that it comes from the past karmas, that one has to pay back by illness the karmas, the actions of the past. I have seen patients go through their illness in the thought that as it is the debt of the past that one has to pay, it is just as well that it should be paid back. When we look at it critically, we find that the one who thinks that it is a punishment that God inflicts upon a person, certainly puts God in a severe light, making Him a hard Judge instead of a most merciful and compassionate Father and Mother, both in one. If the earthly mother and father would not like to inflict pain and suffering upon their child, it is hard to think that God, whose mercy and compassion are infinitely greater than those of the earthly parents, could send illness to a person as a punishment for his actions. It seems more reasonable when a person says that the illness is brought about by his own actions. But it is not always true, it is not true in every case. Very often the most innocent and the best souls, who have nothing but good wishes and kind thoughts, will be found among sufferers.

Thinking that it is the debt of the past life gives one the idea of fatalism, that there is a certain suffering through which one must pass, that there is no other way, and that therefore one must patiently endure something which is most disagreeable. I have seen a young man suffering from an illness, who most contentedly told me, on my giving him advice to do something for his health, 'I believe that this is a debt of the past that I have to pay. I might just as well pay it.' From a business point of view it is very just, but from a spiritual person's point of view it can be looked at differently. What man does not wish for himself is not for him, is not his portion. For in every soul there is the power of the Almighty, there is a spark of divine light, there is the spirit of the Creator; and therefore all that man wishes to have is his birthright. Naturally a soul does not wish to have an illness unless he is unbalanced. If the soul knew the power of his natural inclination to enjoy health, he would experience health in life in spite of all the difficulties that the conditions of life may present.

One may wonder if illness is never to be understood as being the will of God. And if not, how is it with death? Death is different from illness, for illness is worse than death. The sting of death is only momentary; the idea that one leaves one's surroundings is one moment's bitter experience, no longer; but illness is incompleteness, and that is not desirable. Is it wrong to let a person die who is suffering very much, or should one use artificial means to keep him alive? It is not advisable that a doctor, or a relation, or anyone should kill a person who is suffering very much from a disease, in order to save him from pain; for nature is wise, and every moment that one passes on this physical plane has its purpose. We human beings are too limited to judge, to decide to put an end to life and suffering. We must try to make the suffering less for that person, to do everything in our power to make that person feel better. But to use artificial means of keeping someone alive for hours or days is not a right thing to do; because that is going against nature's wisdom and the divine plan. It is as bad as killing a person. The tendency is for man always to go further than he ought to; that is where he makes a mistake.

Can astrology help to find out the cause of a disease? Is such a method to be recommended? Yes, astrology can help to find out the cause, if it is the right astrology; but it is not to be recommended for a person who looks at a condition in which he is helpless. In a case in which it is favourable, it works to his advantage, it is all right; but when it is not favourable, then it works to his disadvantage. For instance an astrologer said to someone, 'In three years' time you will be ill, and in the end you will die.' This man became ill and died at the end of three years. Why must we, therefore, depend upon such things? Why not depend upon the life and light of God which are in us? Why not say to oneself that life lives and death dies? And why not always hope for the best to come, never look at nor expect the worst to come? One might say that in order to be ready to face the worst we should look at the dark side. But by looking at the dark side of things one focuses one's spirit on it, and so involves oneself in all kinds of obscurities, instead of rising above it and seeking for the light, hoping for the best to come. In that way one prepares oneself also to face the worst if it should come.

No doubt a man is very often himself the cause of the disorder of this physical mechanism. It is this disorder which he calls illness, whether it is physical or mental. Sometimes it is his neglect, sometimes an unbalanced condition of his mind or body which causes it; sometimes conditions around him cause an illness. Nevertheless, to have a yielding attitude towards illness is not the right thing. No doubt it is a good thing to look upon the illness of which one has been cured as having been a trial, a test, an ordeal through which one was passing and which one has left behind; thinking that it was for the better, that one is now purified, that one has learned a lesson from it, that one has become more thoughtful and considerate towards oneself and others by an experience like this. To think, 'What I am going through is something that I must continually bear', is not the right attitude. The attitude should be, 'No, this is not my portion in life. I will not have it, I must not have it. I must rise above it, I must forget it. I must do everything in my power to overcome it, by a thought, by a feeling, by a belief, by a good action, by progress, by a conception, by healing, by whatever method.' There must be no limitation.

Sometimes a person says, 'I believe only in healing, I will not touch medicine, it is material'; that is wrong also. Sometimes a person says, 'I only believe in medicine, I have no faith in healing'; that is wrong, too. To grow towards perfect health, to bring about a cure, one must heal oneself from morning till evening. One should think, 'Every ray of the sun cures me, the air heals me; the food I take has an effect upon me; with every breath I inhale something which is healing, purifying, bringing me to perfect health.' With a hopeful attitude towards a cure, towards health, towards a perfect life, a person rises above disorders, which are nothing but inharmonious conditions of mind or body, and makes himself more fit to accomplish his life's purpose.

It is not selfish to think about one's health. No doubt it is undesirable to be thinking about one's illness all the time, to worry about it, or to be too anxious about it; but to care about one's health is the most religious thing there is, because it is the health of body and mind that enables one to do service to God and to one's fellow-men, by which one accomplishes one's life's purpose. One should think, 'I come from a perfect source and I am bound for a perfect goal. The light of the perfect Being is kindled in my soul. I live, move, and have my being in God; and nothing in the world, of the past or present, has power to touch me if I rise above all.' It is this thought which will make one rise above influences of inharmony and disorder, and will bring a person to the enjoyment of the greatest bliss in life, which is health.

There is a saying in the East that there is one illness for which there is no remedy, and that illness is called *Vahm*, which means imagination. In every illness the imagination plays its rôle. The greater the imagination, the greater becomes that illness. But apart from illness, in every little thing in life imagination makes mischief, exaggerates it, and makes it more difficult to bear. It is not seldom but often that one sees a person feeling tired before he has worked, at the very thought of the work. When working, that tiredness which was imagined before increases still more and before the work is finished the person is exhausted. One will often see that the head of a factory is more tired after two hours' work than the workman who has perhaps worked all day long with the engines; a superintendent of a garden becomes much more tired than the gardener who has been working on the soil all day long. Often a person in the audience becomes much more tired than the singer who has sung the whole programme of the evening. And before having walked so many miles a person may have become tired at the thought of it. Imagination always leads, illness follows.

Imagination is an automatic working of the mind. One can train imagination by training thought. We must make thoughts out of imaginations. There comes a development of mind which shows itself just like the muscular development of the physical body, for each muscle is distinct when a person exercises his body; and so every thought becomes distinct and clear before it is expressed. In that way imagination is developed and trained.

There is no doubt that he who has control over his imagination can master himself and can rise above illness. It always amused me, when seeing a lady who used to give lectures, that when the lecture was still about fifteen days ahead she began to be worried; and as the worry came, then some illness followed, doctors came to examine her, and so it went on. When the day of the lecture came the lady was quite finished. Healers had to see her, occultists had to advise her, astrologers had to make her horoscope in order to tell her she would be successful in her lecture, before she would be ready to go and deliver it.

This is not rare; very often one finds that one exaggerates tiredness, confusion, pain, and trouble, and makes a mountain out of a molehill without knowing it. If that person were told, he would not accept it, would not admit it, yet at the same time it is so. Out of a hundred persons, sufferers from a certain illness, you will find ninety-nine who could be cured if their imagination allowed them to be cured.

With children pain increases with imagination, and therefore the one who understands this can stop the pain of a child more quickly than by any medicine, for the child is responsive to suggestion. A grown-up person who holds his imagination in hand and does not let it loose, is difficult to help, but a child can be helped in a moment. A child may be crying in pain, and in a moment's time, if you can get its imagination away from it, you can cure it. A fear of illness comes upon many even before they have felt the pain, if a physician has told them that there is something wrong with them. The physician may be mistaken, yet the fear of the pain that is anticipated takes the place of the disease. With the mentally deranged imagination is the main reason at the back of their illness.

This does not mean that one should overlook the illness of a child. That is another thing. One should neither overlook the illness of a child nor the complaint one has oneself, for it is not always imagination. But at the same time imagination plays a great rôle, and it is better for a person to analyse to what extent imagination plays a part in his complaint. And he may analyse it by trying to forget his pain, to forget it entirely, by trying to deny facts which stand before him as an evidence of illness. When a person is able to do so to that extent, then he will be able to realize how much of it is illness and how much imagination. He will also observe this phenomenon: that as soon as he withdraws his imagination from his illness, he starves his illness of the food which maintains it; and it is possible that by this starvation illness will die. One must not overlook children's illnesses, but at the same time one must not exaggerate, one must not think too much about it; because imagination has a living effect, imagination can create an illness in a person who has not really got one; and it would be a great mistake on the part of the parents to worry over children's health when it is not necessary.

The body comprises a nervous system which is the main mechanism of one's physical body; and this mechanism is much more responsive to imagination than is flesh, bone, or skin. The nerves instantly respond to the thought, not skin, flesh, or bone; these only partake of the influence coming from the nerves. The nervous system stands between the physical and mental aspects of being. Therefore, just as imagination can cause an illness and can maintain an illness, so imagination can also cure a person of illness. Once illness is cured by imagination, what is left of that illness in the body has no sustenance upon which to exist and therefore it naturally dies out. I have often made an experiment with a person who said he had got a very bad headache. I have asked him to sing, and in the end he found that he was cured. Anything that takes the mind away from the imagination of the illness cuts down the props that support that illness; then the illness cannot stand on its feet. There must be something to hold it, and that is imagination.

Self-pity is the worst enemy of man. Although sometimes it gives a tender sensation in the heart to say, 'Oh, how poorly I am', and it is soothing to hear from someone, 'Oh, I am so sorry you are not well', yet I should think that one would prefer if another thing were said in sympathy, namely, 'I am so happy to see you are so well'. In order to create that tender sensation one need not be ill; what is needed is to be thankful. We can never be too thankful. If we can appreciate the privileges of life there are endless gifts from above which we never think about and we never value. If we think of them thankfully, naturally a tenderness is felt; and it is that tenderness which is worth having.

The animal is more responsive to nature than man, and nature helps the animal to forget its illness more than it does man, because man is not responsive to nature. Every man has his little world; it may be so little sometimes that it is like a doll's house; and in that world he lives. He is not conscious of the wide world, he is not conscious of the universe; he just lives in his small world; that is all he knows, that is all he is conscious of, that is all he is interested in. And, therefore, if his world is full of misery and illness and ill-luck, he cannot get out of it, because he has made a kind of shell, as creatures in the water make a shell to live in. The world does not hold misery for him; he has made the shell of misery for himself and he likes to hide in that shell. Because he has made it he likes to live in it, it is his home, be it a shell of wickedness, of misery, of goodness, of piety, or anything else.

Because of outward evidences, a person very often builds up concentration on an illness, for no doubt there are outer signs of illness; but the mind has such a great power that if there is one sign of illness, the mind sees a thousand signs of illness. For instance, as soon as you begin to think that your friend is displeased with you, everything he does, either good or bad, seems to you to have gone all wrong; and if you think your friend is loving and kind to you, all that he does seems to support your thought.

When a person begins to think he is under an unlucky star, with everything that happens, good or bad, he will think, 'It all brings bad luck to me. From everywhere bad luck seems to be coming.' Even a good thing that person will believe to be bad, because he is looking at it in that way. And when a person is living in the thought that good luck is coming to him, everything that comes is in the form of good luck.

The more we study this question, the more we find that our mind is the master of life; and we become the possessor of the Kingdom of God as soon as we have realized the power of thought and concentration upon our life. It is because of the absence of such knowledge that one does not value that divine spark which is in oneself; and by being unconscious of it one goes down and down, till one reaches the deepest depths. No sooner has one realized this than one begins to respect oneself; and it is the self-respecting person who has respect for another, it is the one who helps himself who will help another, it is the one who can raise himself who will take another person also towards the heights. Once we have found the remedy to cure this disease which comes from the imagination, then there is no other disease which we cannot manage to get above; we only have to realize the source of perfection within ourselves.

<hr>

A regular life, pure diet, good sleep, a balance between activity and repose, and right breathing, all these help one to health; but the best remedy for healing oneself of all illnesses and infirmities of mind is belief. Many think that they believe, but there are very few who really believe. The belief of many is as I heard someone say, 'I believe, may God strengthen my belief.' It is an affirmation which has no meaning. If a person says, 'I believe', that does not mean that he believes, for belief in its perfection becomes faith. And what does Christ say about faith? He says, 'Faith removes mountains.' No doubt the priest speaks of faith in the Church, the clergyman of faith in the Book; but that is not the real meaning of faith. Faith is the culmination of belief, and when faith is attained to a certain degree it will grow as a plant. When belief is complete it turns into faith. Cure is brought about by faith in all cases, whether it be a sudden cure or whatever may be the nature and character of the case. Faith speeds the condition; so great as the faith is, so quick the time of healing. Without faith even medicine cannot help. No treatment can give good results where faith is lacking. Faith is the first remedy; everything else comes afterwards. All our failures, sorrows, disappointments, difficulties in life are caused by our lack of belief. Illness means lack of belief. Beyond and above all other evidences illness is the sign of the lack of belief; if one believed, there would certainly be no place for illness. But illness takes the place of belief. One cannot disbelieve in what one believes. Illness becomes one's belief; that is where the difficulty comes in. When a person says, 'I am fighting against my illness', that means, 'My imagination is fighting against my belief.' He affirms, 'I am fighting against my illness', which means he establishes illness in himself. He fights against something which he affirms to be existing. In his belief he gives the first place to the illness; the second place in his belief he gives to the imagination of curing it. Thus the power with which he wishes to remove his illness is much smaller than the power which is already established in him by illness. He fights against something which he affirms to be existing.

There are people who think that they will never fall into such an error as believing in something for which there is no evidence, and they think this is very clever. And when we search in the world of evidences, we shall find one deluding cover under another. And so one can go on, probing the depths of life, from one illusion to another, never arriving at the realization of truth. How can you rely upon evidences which are subject to change? Therefore if there is anything to rely upon it is belief. It is not evidence which gives one belief; and if evidence gives belief, that belief will not last, for evidences are not lasting. It is that belief which stands above evidence which in the end will culminate in faith. It is people like Bayazid, whom many would consider 'in the clouds', who prove in their lives what belief means. Bayazid was going on pilgrimage to Mecca. A dervish was sitting by the way on his journey. Wanting to pay homage to a spiritual man, he went to that dervish and sat down to receive his blessing. The dervish asked him, 'Where are you going?' He said, 'I am going to Mecca.' 'On business?' He was astonished. 'No, on a pilgrimage.' 'On a pilgrimage? What do they do on the pilgrimage?' Bayazid replied, 'They walk around the holy stone of Ka'ba.' The dervish said, 'You do not need to go so far for that pilgrimage. If you will make circles round me and go back your pilgrimage is done.' Bayazid said, 'Yes, I believe this.' He circled around the man and went back home; and when people asked, 'Did you make a pilgrimage to the Ka'ba?' he said, 'Yes, I made a pilgrimage to a living Ka'ba.'

Belief is not an imagination, belief is a miracle in itself, for belief is creative. For instance a person certainly believes that he can get so many centimes for a franc, and everyone believes it, because there is evidence. He has not far to go for the evidence. He has only to go to the bank to find out. But belief is difficult when there is no evidence. It is just like building a castle in the air, but then that castle becomes paradise. If one believes in what does not exist, the belief will make it exist; if there is a condition that one believes in, even if that condition does not exist, it will be produced. The difference between the mind of the believer and the mind of the unbeliever is this, that the mind of the believer is like a torch and the mind of the unbeliever is like a light which is covered by something which does not allow it to spread its light.

Very often a man is afraid of losing his common sense. He would rather be ordinary than become extraordinary. He is afraid of losing himself, but he does not know that losing himself means gaining himself. A person may say, 'To think about these things is like moving in the air.' But if we were not in the air what would become of us? Air is the substance on which we live, more important for us than the food we eat and the water we drink. Belief, therefore, is the food of the believer; it is the sustenance of his faith. It is on belief that he lives, not on food and water.

Faith is so sacred that it cannot be imparted, it must be discovered within oneself; but there is no one in the world who is without faith, it is only covered up. And what covers it? A kind of pessimistic outlook on life. There are people who are pessimistic outwardly, there are others who are pessimistic unconsciously, they themselves do not know that they are pessimistic. Man can fight with the whole world, but he cannot fight with his own self, he cannot break his own doubts; and the one who can disperse these clouds has accomplished a great thing in the world.

Is faith attainable by perseverance in belief? Things of heaven cannot be attained by perseverance, they are the grace of God. No perseverance is required to ask for the grace of God, to believe in the grace of God, and to open oneself for the grace of God, to trust in it. It is this which strengthens belief into faith. Everything belonging to the earth costs us more or less, we purchase it; there is only one thing which does not cost anything, because we can never pay its price, and that is the grace of God. We cannot pay for it in any form, in any way, by our goodness, by our piety, by our great qualities, merits or virtues, nothing. For what does our goodness amount to? Our lifelong goodness is nothing more than a drop of water compared with the sea. We as human beings are too poor to pay for the grace of God in order to purchase it; it is only given to us.

For God is love. What do we expect from love? Grace. The grace of God is the love of God, love of God manifesting in innumerable blessings, blessings which are known and unknown to us. Human beings live on earth in their shells, mostly unaware of all the privileges of life, and therefore ungrateful to the Giver of them. In order to see the grace of God one must open one's eyes, raising one's head from the little world that one makes around oneself, and thus see above and below, right and left, before and behind, the grace of God reaching one from everywhere in abundance. If one tries to thank, one might thank for thousands of years and it would never be enough. But if one looks in one's own little shell one does not find the grace of God; what one finds is miseries, troubles, difficulties, injustice, hard-heartedness, coldness of the world, all ugliness from everywhere. Because when a person looks down he sees mud, but when he looks up there are beautiful stars and planets. It only depends which way one looks, upwards or downwards. What is this mortal world? What is this physical existence? What is this life of changes? If it were not for belief, what use is it all? Something which is changing, something which is not reliable, something which is liable to destruction. Therefore it is not only for the sake of truth, but for life itself that one must find belief in oneself, develop it, nurture it, allow it to grow every moment of one's life, that it may culminate in faith. It is that faith which is the mystery of life, the secret of salvation.

# Part

## 2

# Healing

# 1
# The Main Aspects of Healing

## Balance

HEALTH depends upon the balance between activity and repose in the five senses: sight, smell, hearing, taste, and touch; and every sense, in the normal condition of health, must be able to express itself and to respond. The senses need more time for repose than for activity. Therefore the mystics go into seclusion in order to give a chance of repose to the senses, which are different in every man. Everyone passes every moment of his waking state in activity of the senses, partly by intention, partly involuntarily. For instance, the eyes look at things intentionally perhaps a hundred times a day, but nine hundred times they look at things without intention. This shows a waste of energy in an average man's life.

In order to develop healing power one must regulate and control the senses by regulating their activity and repose; and this, done with a spiritual thought, converts power of mind into divine power. A person can heal with power of mind alone, but the results will be limited; but a person with divine power can obtain through it unlimited results.

It depends on the condition of the health how much activity one can stand and how much repose is necessary; a general rule cannot be made for everyone. A normal amount of activity stimulates and strengthens the body. Therefore physical exercises are given for physical development, and exercises of concentration and studies are given for the development and repose of the mind. According to psychic law the day is natural for activity and the night for repose, and when this is not carried out it naturally works against health. It is not necessary to rest after every little exertion, but a degree of balance ought to be maintained; and it is advisable in life to take repose without allowing it to develop into laziness.

### Breath

Breath is the principal and essential power that can help in healing. There is a silent healing, and a healing by focusing the glance, by holding the painful part with the fingers, by rubbing it, by waving the hand over the painful part, by touching and by not touching it; but behind these different ways there is one power working, and that is the power of the breath. This power can be developed by breathing practices, and when the breath is so developed that it creates an atmosphere around the healer, then the very presence of the healer heals. The power of the breath can be developed by physical exercises, by rhythmic exercises of the breath, by pure living and by concentration.

The power of healing is greater than the power of the channels one uses to heal, such as the finger-tips or eyes. The eyes have more power than the finger-tips. They are finer, and the power that manifests through them is radiant, while it is not so radiant in the finger-tips. But besides the power of healing one must have a clear idea of how to recognize the complaint of another person and of the best way to heal him.

### Healing with the Fingertips

Hygiene is the first subject to consider in healing with the tips of the fingers. Hands that have been engaged in any work or that are stained with any liquid must be washed for healing. The healer must first observe the hygienic rules of keeping his body, as well as his clothes, pure and clean; especially at the time of healing he must be absolutely free from all that is unhygienic. The sleeves, at the time of healing, must be rolled back, and the finger-nails must be clean and properly trimmed. After healing one should wave the hand, as it were shaking it, to shake off any fine atoms, or even vibrations, so that a poison taken from the painful part of the patient may not be given to the patient again.

There are cases in which the sensation of the body is deadened by the pain, and the pain has gone into the depth of the affected part of the body. In such cases waving the hand or touching is not enough, rubbing is necessary. When dealing with the effects of poison from the sting of a bee or scorpion, or from snake-bite or the bite of any other poisonous animal, a simple soft touch or stroking of the affected part is indicated; if the pain is more intense touch is not necessary, simply the waving of the hand close to the affected part. In the case of the bite of a mad dog one should put some lime mixed with water on a copper coin and tie it on the part that the teeth have touched, and the rest of the affected part must be healed by touching and stroking it with the tips of the fingers. Bites of mosquitoes and midges may be cured by applying butter that has been boiled and allowed to cool, and then waving the hand over the affected part. Rose-water may be used for bites of all kinds, in cases of severe inflammation.

### The Tracing of Disease

The healer's work in tracing disease is subtler than healing; for in healing power is necessary, but in tracing the disease—its nature, its cause, its secret—psychic power is of no use, there inspiration is needed; and a healer without this is an incomplete healer. The patient generally does not know the real cause, nature, and secret of his complaint. He is not supposed to know; for the patient knows the effect of the poison, not its cause, nature, and secret. The healer must trace the patient's complaint from his face, expression, voice, work, and movement; everything tells. Sometimes the healer must find out the cause by asking the patient the details about his pain and the circumstances of his life, and by knowing the attitude and the inclination of the patient.

The secret of disease can be traced also by observing what a person desires in the way of food and clothing, and in what environments he prefers to be, what attitude he has towards his friends and foes, his choice of sweet and savoury and his attraction to colours. For instance a person with a complaint that originates from melancholy will have a liking for purple; a person who has lost control over his passions will show an inclination towards passion, and he will generally like red; a person who is lifeless, who has an inclination to emptiness, will have a tendency towards white; a person who has gone through a sorrow and mourned over things and weakened his heart by it, will have an inclination towards black.

So it is with sweet and savoury: the patient who shows an inclination for sweet shows weakness of heart, and by that general weakness; and the patient who shows inclination towards savoury lacks circulation.

There are many things in the patient that one can perceive not only from his inclinations but by noticing his face and features; for in this way one reads more than by any other method. The features tell his general characteristics, and therefore a person knows the weakness that may have been the origin of his complaint, and the general expression shows the thought behind it. Since mind is the cause of all causes, the healer gets at the root of the complaint as soon as he touches the mind of the patient. How true is the saying, man's face is the mirror of his heart.

## The Chief Reason of Every Disease

According to the mystical point of view there is one chief root, which can be called a common cause, from which all diseases are derived, and that is disorder of rhythm. The upset of the nerves is stated by scientists to be the chief origin of all mental diseases, and their effect upon the body produces various diseases in the body. Religious people teach concentration and meditation, sitting in a prayerful attitude. The wisdom behind all this is to bring the activity of mind and body to a normal condition. For it is the nature of activity to become more active every moment; it is the activity itself that produces energy, and the consequence is that by so producing energy, its own strength throws it out of its normal rhythm.

This one can see in the burning of the fire. The activity is little at the start; but with every moment that it burns its activity increases and culminates in the end in its utmost speed. And the speed of the beginning compared with the speed of the end will prove that it is the increase of speed of the fire which has brought about the climax, when it consumes itself. In human nature we see the same tendency. When speaking one is inclined to speak more and more quickly, until the speed is so increased that one leaves out several words of the sentence without any intention of doing so. So it is in walking; the pace increases with every step until a person finds himself almost running. So it is with the imagination, and sometimes one sees the same thing with the pulsation of the body and the circulation of the blood. Uncontrolled increase of speed, in all its aspects, hastens the climax, and when unbalanced culminates in disastrous results.

A healer without this knowledge is a blind healer who does not know the cause of diseases; his healing is a chance; but the one who knows this is more than a physician and more than a healer. He will control his own activity, and the power of control thus gained will enable him to control the activity of others, in order to keep it normal, in which is the true health of mind and body.

## The Reason for Tiredness

Tiredness is due to three causes: loss of energy which is the chief reason, and besides this excess of activity of mind and of body. One generally knows tiredness to be caused by excess of bodily activity, but one is apt to overlook the fact that excess of activity of mind also causes tiredness.

The activities that specially cause tiredness are worry, fear, anxiety, and pain. There is, however, one mental cause that is less obvious, and that is the thought of being tired. Among a hundred cases of tired people you will find ninety cases of this particular kind of tiredness. When a person thinks, 'I am tired', the very thought creates the feeling of tiredness in support of the thought, and reason brings forward a thousand reasons that seem to have caused the tiredness. There are some who think that the presence of people or of some people, or the presence of a particular person, tires them; some think that their energy, their life, is eaten up by some people; some think that a particular action takes away their energy; some think that their strength is taken out of them by their everyday duty in life or the work they happen to do, such as singing, speaking, doing bodily or mental work; and of course, as they think so they experience.

In truth, there is no doubt that every kind of activity must take away some energy, more or less. But by one's thought one

increases the loss; by preserving the energy and using it economically one saves it to a great extent. And there is one way, which is a spiritual way, in which one can give out energy with every activity that necessitates one's giving it out, yet at the same time one can absorb much more energy than one loses, from the life within, without, around, and about one. It is for this reason that religion has given the conception of God being almighty. Those who consider Him to be far away in heaven keep away from Him, but those who realize the meaning of the teaching in the Bible that 'we live and move and have our being in God', feel Him at all times by their side. If consciousness of wealth makes one feel rich, and if consciousness of strength makes one feel strong, how much stronger and richer should he feel who is really God-conscious!

### Balance

A healer often finds patients whose complaints may differ and yet may have originated in lack of balance. Balance is the most difficult thing in life to keep for anybody and everybody. Many times a healer succeeds in curing a patient by just showing him some practices by which he can attain balance. This, besides healing, brings about a most desirable effect. Balance is gained in different ways, even in ordinary actions such as sitting, lying, standing, and walking; standing with even weight on both legs, sitting cross-legged, or on one's heels, both carrying an equal part of the weight of the body; also kneeling, walking rhythmically with an even force given to the swing of both arms. By regularity of eating and drinking, working and resting, sleeping and rising, one gets balance too. The first thing a healer should consider when treating a patient is that he must give him balance.

# Pain

Pain has two origins: the mind and the body. Sometimes it is caused by the mind and held by the body, and sometimes it is caused by the body and held by the mind. If one were absent or did not partake of the pain suggested by the other part of the being, the pain would not exist, or if it existed it would vanish. The body being the servant of the mind, can never refuse to bear the pain given by the mind, having no free will of its own; it is only the mind that could refuse, if it were trained to do so.

The doctrine that some people hold that there is no such thing as pain, is very helpful in the training of the mind, although its truth may be questioned. If it is true that there is no such thing as pain, it can only be true in the sense that everything in this world is an illusion, it has no existence of its own, it does not exist in reality, compared with the ultimate reality that is. But when a person says that it is only pain which does not exist, but that joy exists and all other things exist, then he is wrong.

Among Sufis dervishes have tried to become pain-proof by inflicting upon themselves cruel injuries, such as whipping the bare arms or cutting the muscles of the body, or piercing the body with knives, or taking the eyes out of their sockets and replacing them in their sockets again, which I have seen myself. By this they have discovered a truth and have given it to the thinking world: that the mind can refuse to partake of the bodily pain, and by so doing the bodily pain is felt much less than it would otherwise be. When the mind goes forward to receive bodily pain, out of fear or self-pity, it increases the pain and makes it much more than it would otherwise be. The proportion that fear or self-pity add to the pain is ninety-five per cent. And the first thing that the healer must do in curing patients suffering from pain, is to erase the pain from the surface of the patient's mind by suggestion and also by his healing power. In the absence of support on the part of the mind, the body must give up pain, for it has no power to hold it any longer without the mind.

## Healing by Medicine

Very often it happens that a healer or a believer in healing goes to such an extreme that he does not accept healing by medicine. In reality the thought of being given medicine by a doctor and the thought of repeating the treatment he has prescribed so many times a day, apart from its medicinal influence, is psychically helpful; and the healers of the East, considering this, have to a certain extent played the part of a physician also. With their healing power, spiritual, psychic, and magnetic, with their hypnotic suggestion and with their mesmeric influence, they gave the patient something to eat or to drink in the form of medicine. Sometimes they gave a charm to keep by him and sometimes magnetized water.

The idea is that man is more conscious of the objective world and its activity than of any other plane of existence, and by eating or drinking, or by holding or possessing a certain thing the impression upon him becomes more real. The thought of the healer, which should ease the mind, is often hindered when the external senses of the patient are not fully responsive to it; but when the patient eats or drinks something, or tastes something, or feels something applied to or touching the painful part, the senses become the medium for the healer's thought to reach the mind of the patient. Knowledge of the physical medium is most essential for a healer, for every psychic operation requires a medium, and through a distinct and responsive medium every psychical work meets with success.

# 2
# The Psychological
# Nature of Diseases

## Causes of Diseases

THE PSYCHOLOGICAL nature of diseases can be explained in a few words as being the lack of life, either because of insufficient matter in the body, or because of excess of matter which leaves no scope for the spirit; it is also the impression of pain which the mind holds. Pain is not always physical. There are physical causes; but as soon as the mind knows of discomfort, out of fear it holds it; and this is called pain.

Disease is often caused by lack of rhythm, be it in thought or feeling, in the breath, in action, or in one's everyday life. For instance, to stay up in the night when one is accustomed to sleep, to change the dinner-hour, to take a nap when one is not accustomed to, to do anything that one is not accustomed to do, puts one out of rhythm. People who are accustomed to be angry or to quarrel would become ill if they were not allowed to do that. There is a story told in India that a person who could not keep any secret was compelled to keep quiet; in the end he became ill, and the doctor had to cure him by permitting him to let it out. All this signifies rhythm; every habit forms a rhythm.

The fear of catching a disease is also a cause of illness. There are people who wonder if they are ill, and try to find out if there is something wrong with them. There are some who enjoy self-pity or the sympathy of others; these invite disease. Some entertain disease when they are to a certain extent unwell. They wish to be treated like a patient, or try to take to a lazy life. By so doing, the mind naturally holds the disease longer, since it is allowed to do so.

There are many other causes of illness. Among them the most unfortunate is the impression: 'I have got an illness that can never be cured', for this impression is worse than a disease. In reality the soul of every individual, healthy or ill, is pure from any pain or disease, and it constantly heals mind and body, and if it were not for the mind and body, which create illness, a person would always be well. It is natural to be healthy; and all illness, pain, and discomfort are unnatural.

### Magnetic Power

The health of both mind and body depends upon a magnetic power which may be called in metaphysical terms the power of affinity in elements and in atoms. It may be pictured as scattered grains of rice united by being attracted to one another; and it is this power which attracted them and shaped them into a certain form. Both mind and body are made of atoms; the former of mental atoms, the latter of physical atoms; and the power that gathered them and made them into one body or one mind is the magnetic power.

Lack of this power causes all pain, discomfort, and disease, while development of this power secures health of body and mind. By physical practices this power is developed in the body, and by mental exercises the same power is improved in the mind. It is generally found that the ill lose their magnetism to a certain extent. A healthy person often seeks to escape from the presence of the sick. It is natural, because it is magnetism in a person to which mankind is attracted, and it is its lack which causes repulsion. This also explains the reason for the attraction of youth and childhood, although in childhood this magnetism is not fully developed. The lack of this is felt in age for the same reason.

In Sufi terms this magnetism is called *Quwwat-e-Maknatis*; and it springs from every atom, physical or mental. It may be called strength or energy. It is a wealth; and just as one person can enjoy wealth for a longer time if he is careful with it, and another may spend it thoughtlessly following his fancies, so does a man do with this magnetism. Either he attracts others or he is attracted to others. In one case he is better off, in the other case he loses. Man, of whatever evolution, whatever disposition, in whatever condition of life, needs this magnetism more than anything else; for health, which is the greatest of all gifts in life, depends greatly on magnetism.

### Breathing

In Sanskrit breath is called *Prana*, which means life. This prana not only gives life to oneself but it gives life to another person too. Sometimes the presence of someone fills you with life, and sometimes the presence of another so to speak takes away your life from you. One feels tired and depressed and eaten up by the presence of one person, and another person's presence gives added strength, life, and vigour. This is all accounted for by the breath. The one who has more life gives life, while the one who has less life takes it from the one who has more. But there is a contrary process too. Sometimes the stronger one takes away what little life is left in the weaker one, and sometimes the weaker one gives out his life to the stronger one. A person who takes away life in fact absorbs the life from another. In the presence of that person even flowers fade sooner and plants die.

Many deaths occur and many lives are retained by the pheno-

mena of the breath. Therefore for the healer there is no greater source of healing. He can throw his breath upon the affected part of the patient as easily as he can cast his glance upon a painful part. Even eatables and objects that a healer's breath has magnetized carry with them the power of healing. If touch makes certain finger-marks through perspiration upon a thing, why should not the breath, the very essence of life, live in an object and give the object some greater part of life, producing in it an effect which may be a greater cure than medicine?

When the breath is developed and purified it is not necessary for the healer even to make an effort to throw his breath upon the patient, but the atmosphere that his breath creates, the very presence of the healer brings about a cure, for the whole atmosphere becomes charged with magnetism.

## Insanity

There are no doubt many physical causes of various aspects of insanity, but a keen study of the subject will prove that insanity is mostly due to mental causes. Some lack of balance caused by the intensity or excess of a certain thought and feeling is found to be at the root of every cause of insanity. The physician fails to cure such cases, especially he who traces the cause of insanity in its outer manifestations and in the physical body. Every cause has an external effect, and yet it is a mistake to take the effect for the cause. It is not generally medicine or even surgical operations or any external applications that can be of great use. It is more the work of a healer than of a physician to cure insanity.

Like every disease, insanity could easily be cured in its earlier stage, and it is again the work of the healer to recognize the signs of insanity in their primary state; for mostly such signs are not noticed in a person, or they are passed over as 'something funny' or 'queer'. The first step towards healing insanity is to get at the root of the complaint by association with the subject; and as soon as the root of the complaint is touched a great relief is brought, even before healing. Naturally, insanity being a mental disease, thought-power alone is the remedy for it.

Loss of memory, confusion, puzzlement, instantaneous temper and passion, all these are signs of the beginning of insanity. Insanity is inherited from the family, but it can also be traced in several weaknesses and vices, among which drink and fondness for drugs, unnatural habits, too much worry, anxiety, and allowing melancholy thoughts to develop in the nature; these are all things that cause insanity.

The work of the healer is first to detect the primary indication of insanity, and that is loss of memory. It is caused by weakness of the mind. The mind has not sufficient power to bring forward the thought entrusted to it at the command of the will. It is this which may be called loss of memory, and it must be healed and cured in its very beginning. The primary stage is marked by an extreme activity of mind which results in extreme thoughtless anger or passion; then when its spell is passed repentance comes. This should be avoided at its beginning. Guilty conscience, fear of consequences, doubting tendencies, all such things are like fuel to the fire of insanity. A pure, thankful, useful life, a constant thought of appreciating things and avoiding blaming things and people and conditions, all these help to keep away the germ of insanity.

## Spirit

There is a part of one's life which can only be called life; there is no other name appropriate for it, and the English phrase, 'to pull oneself together', means to set that part of life to work. It might be called spirit, as this part in itself is both intelligence and power. It is intelligence because any part of the body and mind or every part of both in which it dwells, it makes sensitive; and it is powerful because whatever part of the body and mind it touches, it strengthens that part.

In games and sports, when people jump down from a great height, what is it that protects them from hurt? It is this spirit, and they have made it their habit to call this spirit to their aid. When people throw balls to each other, and even in boxing, the receiver of the blow awakens this spirit in that part on which he receives the blow. The sportsman does not know what this spirit is, though he takes refuge in it. The mystic understands it by his meditation, also by research into metaphysics. When a person awakes from a deep sleep, the first thing that rises through his mind to his body, when the tendency of stretching and contracting comes and of twisting and turning, and of gradually opening the eyes, is this spirit; it rises, so to speak, and spreads.

By the mastery of this spirit diseases are cured, age is mastered, even death is conquered. When this spirit is lacking, energy is lacking, intelligence, joy, and rest are lacking, and when there is this spirit there is hope, there is joy, there is rest; because the nature of this spirit is to hold intact the body of atoms and vibrations. Comfort lies in its being held, discomfort when that spirit is not sufficient to hold the body intact. Thus it is the lack of this spirit that is the cause of a great many diseases. By the development of this spirit in himself the healer can give a part of his spirit to another, and that becomes the best source of healing.

## The Origin of Diseases

Almost every disease originates in the mind, even when one catches infectious diseases. It does not mean that it must always be wickedness of the mind; if it were so good people would never be ill; and yet it cannot be overlooked that it is a weakness of the mind, in some way or other, that allows the disease to enter. Besides this, negligence, oversight, irregularity, mental and physical, also cause diseases. Life and death are two forces, constructive and destructive, and there is continual fighting between these two forces. There are times when one power wins, and the success of that power means either better health or disease and death. The body must be ready and fit to fight this battle; but the mind has a still greater part to perform, and when the mind fails to perform its part the body with all its fitness is incapable of retaining health. But if the mind is capable of keeping health, the body to a great extent obeys it. Still, harmony of both mind and body is needed to fight the battle of life.

## The Effects of Food

It is the secret of nature that life lives upon life, as all carnivorous animals live on the flesh of other animals, and sometimes on their own kind. This shows that life sustains its body by the same element of which it is made. Man's body is made of the food he eats, and it is according to the life in the food he eats that his life develops. Little insects which live on flowers create the beauty of the flower in their body. Insects that are fed on leaves sometimes become green and beautiful like a leaf, but insects living in the earth and in dirt have a similar body. This teaches that man's body depends upon the food he eats. Any decay in the vegetables he eats and any disease in the animal whose flesh he uses, all have their effect on man's health.

Brahmins, who have been the most scientific and philosophical people in the world, have always considered this subject; and one always finds in the race of Brahmins intelligent and superior minds. In the West, although there is continual scientific discovery and discussion on hygienic life, important things in regard to food are overlooked, and this can be explained in a few words as due to the lack of home-life. Many have to take their food in public places where it is impossible for special consideration to be given in this way. There are, moreover, differences in the animal foods one eats. Some animals are clean, others unclean; and their flesh differs accordingly. This has a great influence on the health and the mind of a person.

The question as to what the mind has to do with bodily food may be answered thus, that as an alcoholic drink has an effect on the mind, so every atom of food even has a particular effect. There are foods of three kinds: Sattwa which gives nourishment with calm and peace; Rajas which gives stimulus to work and move about; and Tammas which gives sleep, laziness, and confusion.

A healer must become aware of all kinds of foods and their effects so as to prescribe for the patient, and to see whether the food is the cause of the illness, which is so in many cases, and to keep himself in such a condition that he may be able to heal successfully.

## Self-Control

There are many people who may be said to be of nervous temperament; who have a tendency if they walk to walk quickly, if they work to work hurriedly, if they talk to talk fast, so fast that they may drop words and make the hearer confused; whose temper may rise suddenly and who are inclined to laugh or to cry easily. This condition in a way gives a kind of joy, but it weakens a person and takes away his self-control, and in the end this results in nervous diseases. It begins as indulgence in activity and ends in weakness. Many mental diseases are caused by this negative state of mind and body. From childhood there is an inclination to this, especially among children of nervous temperament; and if it can be checked at that time there is a sure result. No disease can be worse than an increasing weakness of the nerves, which is lack of self-control; for life is not worth living when control over the self is lost.

## Man's Being

Man is not only constituted of matter in his being but also of spirit. However well built a body he may have with its mechanism in good working order, there is still something that is wanting in him. For the physical body is sustained by material food and drink, breath by the air, mind by thoughts and imaginations and impressions; but that is not all, there is something besides mind and body that man possesses in his being, and that is his spirit, which is light, a divine light. It is for this reason that sunshine makes one feel bright; but it is not only sunshine that is needed for the spirit. Man's soul is like a planet; and as the planet is illuminated by the sun, so man's spirit is illuminated by the light of God. In the absence of this, however healthy and joyful a man may look, he is not really healthy. He must have some spiritual touch, some opening in his heart which will let the light come in, the light of God.

## 3
## The Development
## of Healing Power

### The Breath

THE BREATH is the principal power needed in healing. All the various manifestations of the magnetic current which come from the tips of the fingers, from the glance, and from the pores of the skin are indirect manifestations of the breath. It is the strength of breath which gives magnetic power in all its different aspects. Weakness of breath causes weakness of mind and body, and strength of breath is strength to both. One cannot lack energy and magnetism if one's breath is full of energy. Therefore before developing any other means of healing the power of the breath should first be developed.

There are two ways of developing the power of the breath: one way is to make it extensive, and the other way is to make it intensive. After that the breath should be mastered so that it can be directed to any desired part of one's own body; and secondly, it should be mastered so that it may be directed to any side, level, upward, downward, to the right or to the left. Just as one becomes master of aim when one is able to hit the target at any point, so one must master the breath.

There are Yogis in India who can put out a light at some distance by the power of the breath; and even the miracle of Tansen, who is said to have lighted candles by the power of his song when he sang the Dipak, can be nothing else but the power of breath in its fullest development.

## Purification

Science has always admitted, and values every day more highly, the importance of cleanliness around the patient and on the part of the physician; and things of different kinds have been used as disinfectants in many cases of disease. The healer, who has to do more with the mind, must, therefore, realize how very important it is to consider purity of mind as well as of body for the purpose. No doubt it is difficult after learning the nature of things to say which is pure and which is impure; but one way of understanding it is that everything in itself is pure, and when another element is mixed with it, then its purity is polluted. Deep thought in this direction would open a vast field to a thinker.

Another way of understanding the pure and impure is that there is one thing alone that keeps things pure, and that is life, and when the life is gone out of them they are impure. There is a third way of looking at it: that death is impurity of things, but destruction is their purity. This also opens a vast scope of understanding to an observant student of life.

In short, it is necessary for a healer to observe the laws of hygienic life and to keep himself from taking the germs of disease from the patients he heals. Besides, he should avoid all thoughts of bitterness, ill-will, wrath, anger, jealousy, purify his mind from all spite or malice, and bathe so to speak in devotion to God, so that his heart may become saturated with mercy and compassion. It is not only the power of mind that heals, but the purity of mind. The mind free from all crookedness, deceit, treachery, is alone capable of emitting power, strong and pure in its nature, which can give to a patient a new life and relieve him from all pain.

# Rhythm

The development of healing power depends upon the development of the breath. The breath can be developed by purification, by extension, by expansion, and by rhythm.

There are three different kinds of rhythm in the breath: the rhythm which cannot be distinguished in the continuation of inhalation and exhalation; the rhythm that can be distinguished by the two distinct swings of inhaling and exhaling; and evenness in breathing. Those who have not mastered their breath are under the influence of these three rhythms, their health, their mood, and their condition in life; but those who master the breath, can put their breath in any of these rhythms; and when mastery is acquired then the healer has the key to wind any clock. In reality every disease means something wrong with the rhythm. As a doctor says congestion is the root of diseases, so to a Sufi congestion means lack of rhythm; it may be in the circulation, in breathing, in activity, or in repose. A physician in order to find a disease examines the pulse, the beats of the heart, and the condition of the lungs. This itself is the proof that rhythm is the keeper of health, and when there is something wrong with the health the rhythm in some way or other has gone wrong, as when the tick of the clock gets out of rhythm the clock goes too fast or too slow, and it does not give the proper time.

The healer, therefore, must get his rhythm right, so that he can control the mechanism of another person's body. In India there is a custom of clapping the hands or snapping the fingers when somebody is yawning. The idea is that yawning is the sign of the falling of the rhythm, it is the rhythm of one's body that falls to a slower rate when one feels inclined to sleep, and the clapping of the hands and the snapping of the fingers set the pulsation of the other person in the same rhythm as before. It is just like shaking a person who is nodding, to bring the mechanism of his body into proper working order. When the healer is capable of regulating his own rhythm he becomes capable also of making another person's rhythm regular. It requires great knowledge and inspiration concerning the nature of the human mind and body; and the healer who knows how to work with it is like the conductor with the orchestra. The health of everyone that he heals he keeps regular, as the conductor keeps the rhythm of every musician who plays in the orchestra.

## The Power of the Breath

It is the power of the breath which heals body and mind, since breath is life, and through the breath life can be imparted to the mind and body of another person. The breath is also a cord that runs through human beings, connecting them in one life. If it were not for the breath the senses would never have perceived the external world. Therefore all that one sees, smells, feels, tastes, and hears is through the channel of the breath, and therefore no medicine can have such influence on a patient as the breath. Weak breath is susceptible to all contagious diseases, and a healer with weak breath could get the disease from his patient in one healing; that is why power of breath is the most essential thing before one should attempt to heal.

Power of breath can be developed in two ways: volume and length, which make it intensive and extensive. It is dangerous to try healing before one is fully sure of the power of the breath in both ways. The development of the power of the breath is felt, and one knows when one is ready to use it in healing.

## One Common Cause of All Diseases

All pain, discomfort, disease, decay, and destruction of every sort are lack of life. The word life which we use in everyday language is the name of the result of two activities working harmoniously: one, the constant life of the spirit; the other the life that matter provides for it. This is a negative and positive activity. It is the power of inner life which attracts outer life to it, and again it is the strength of external life by which it clings to the inner life. In this way the reciprocal action of both keeps the flame of life burning, and the lack of either of these activities is the cause of disease.

There are five bodies through which the soul experiences life, the physical body being the poorest of all, for it is born of matter, fed with matter, attracted to matter, finds its life in matter, and returns to matter. As it demands matter for its sustenance, so matter demands it in the end; this demand is called disease or death when this body loses its strength; and this is caused by the loss of energy of the nerves, which so to speak pull together and keep the flesh, bone, blood, and skin not only intact, but active and vigorous. It is the weakening of these nerves by exhaustion or by lack of sustenance, by lack of rest or by loss of energy in whatever manner, which is the cause of all disease.

Thus healing may be called life-giving to that part that needs life or to the body as a whole. The materialist believes that a person, however weak, can be saved and brought to life by injecting into his body the blood of another. If that is a successful remedy, how much more could the power of thought, of life, which has more power than matter, produce life in another! And even the fine essence of the healer's physical body may be passed through gases by the process of earth rising to water, water to fire, fire to air, air to ether, and sending the finest atoms of physical energy and strengthening vibrations of mental energy to a person who needs it. The difference between medicine and healing is this: instead of sending a thing by railway it is sent through the sky by an aeroplane.

One may ask if it is worth while weakening oneself by giving part of one's life to another. No doubt it would not do for a poor person to give his last penny to one who is starving, but it is the only thing for a rich man to do, to make use of his riches for the comfort and happiness of those who are in need. A spiritual healer is rich with divine strength, and his power will not be lessened if he gives it out. Therefore material healing is a failure. However successful it may seem, it is powerless compared with spiritual healing, because the spiritual healer has the power of God on his side.

## Development of Power in the Fingertips

The human form may be called materialized light, the symbol of which in mysticism is the five-pointed star, suggesting the head, arms, and feet, which make five points. The nature of light is to spread its rays, and as the human form is made of light —Nur—the hands and the feet, the fingers and the toes, the organs of the senses and the hair all represent rays. It is the knowledge of this light that one sees in the Eastern customs of blessing with the tips of the fingers on the head; and of kissing the hand or touching the feet, for the fingers and toes are the source of the radiance.

The healer, therefore, develops the power of the finger-tips. As by directing the breath in a certain way through the body and mouth one can produce a certain pitch on a certain note, so by directing the energy through the finger-tips and by developing the magnetic power of the finger-tips one develops the power of healing. Moses is known to have possessed a light in his palm, which the poets call *Yad-e-baiza**; and Zoroaster is always pictured with burning fire in his hand. Both suggest the

* Baiza means egg; the palm is egg-shaped.

radiance, the battery that can be developed in the human hand. When the power is developed in the palm it pours out from the tips of the fingers and it shoots out when it is directed by the will. Then by magnetic passes and by touch on the painful part the healer is able to cure diseases.

## The Power of the Presence

It must be understood by a healer that his very presence must emit healing power, and in order to do this the healer must have an overflowing life, power, and magnetism. In the first place the body must be healthy, clean, and pure, so that physical magnetism may be beneficial; also purity of mind is necessary, together with sympathy for the patient and a desire to cure him instead of profiting by his cure. The soul speaks most in the form of the atmosphere; in other words, the atmosphere tells what the soul says. The development of the soul is brought about by a spiritual process and spiritual life. Therefore the development of the mind, of the body, and of the soul is necessary in order to possess a healing power and presence.

## The Power of the Mind

The power of concentration is the first thing necessary to develop healing power. The healer must be able to hold steadily the thought for the cure of his patient whenever he requires. Concentration is most difficult, but if this is accomplished, there is nothing that one cannot accomplish. It is useless to try and cure the patient by any process, however successful and good it may be, if there is no power of concentration. The work of the mind in healing is much greater than in anything else, for it is using the power of the mind on matter; and matter, which has been a disobedient slave of the spirit for ages, through the mineral, through the vegetable, and even through the animal kingdom always rebels against being controlled.

No doubt mind can control matter and do with it whatever it likes, but when mind is enfeebled by serving matter, it loses power over matter. If it were not so, every man would cure himself by controlling matter and there would be no need of a healer. One's own power has a greater influence on oneself than the power of another; besides no one can feel so much sympathy for another as one can for oneself. The nature of the mind is to slip from one's grip. Concentration is the practice which enables the mind—which, so to speak, strengthens its own fingers—to hold fast whatever it can hold. Another secret of the mind is that even with the power of concentration the mind does not hold anything that is not interesting, and it is sympathy in the mind which is the stimulus to the holding power of the mind. Therefore no one can be a successful healer unless his sympathy comes forward with its hands extended to raise the patient from his pain.

## The Power of Concentration

Before a person attempts to heal another he must develop in himself the power of concentration. The concentration of a healer should be so developed that not only when sitting in meditation and closing his eyes can he visualize the desired object, but that even with his eyes open he should be able to hold fast the picture that his mind has created in spite of anything that may be before his eyes. In healing it is necessary to know what picture one should hold in one's mind. If the healer should happen to hold the picture of a wound, he would help the wound to continue instead of being healed; and so if he thought of pain it might perhaps be continued more intensely by the help of his thought. It is the cure that he should hold in mind; it is the desired thing that he must think about, not the condition. In all aspects of life this rule must be remembered; that even in trouble one must not think of the trouble and in illness one must forget about illness. Man often continues life's miseries by giving thought to them. The healer must from beginning to end hold the thought of cure and of nothing else.

## Sending Power to a Distance

The greater development in healing power is to be able to send power to a distance. No land nor sea can prevent power being sent by the mind. Scientific discoveries such as wireless telegraphy prove that by means of instruments thoughts can be sent to a distance, but the mystic has always realized and practised to a great extent the sending of thought to a distance. As the whole idea of a mystic is to serve humanity by love and goodness, he naturally does not feel inclined either to prove to the world the greatness of his power or to utilize his power for any worldly end except for healing.

The Hindu metaphysical term Nada Brahma, meaning sound-God, explains the secret of life, that sound is motion and therefore nothing takes place unless first moved by some force behind. As for external action a physical movement is necessary, so for a mental action the motion must be caused by one's mind. The voice of one person may reach to the other corner of the room, and the voice of another may reach to the other end of the street, and so it is with the power of the mind. As it is necessary to develop the power of the voice by practice, so it is necessary to develop and practise the power of the mind, but it should be remembered that the gift of healing is always necessary. A gifted person may progress much further and more quickly than a person without the gift.

There are three things necessary in sending thought to a distance: first, faith in the theory; second, self-confidence, meaning confidence in one's own power; third, the power of concentration. However great the power of concentration may be, without self-confidence it is of no use; and self-confidence without faith in the theory is powerless. Healing at a distance is the last stage at which a healer arrives after long experience in healing, and attempting this at the beginning would naturally result in failure. Work gives experience, and experience gives confidence; and faith becomes firm when it is built by experience and strengthened by confidence.

# 4
# The Application of Healing Power

## Healing by Charms

THERE is a great power hidden in the mystery of the repetition of a sacred word, but there is a still greater power in writing a sacred word; because the time taken to write a sacred word carefully is perhaps five times or ten times as long as the time taken to repeat a sacred word. Besides, action completes the thought-power better than speech. In writing a sacred name it is the completing of a thought which is even more powerful than uttering the word. But when a person thinks, feels, speaks, and writes, he has developed the thought through four stages and made it powerful. Sufis, therefore, give a charm to the faithful who they think believe in the healing power of the charm. They call it *Taviz*. The patient keeps it with him night and day, and links his thought with the thought of the healer, and feels at every moment that he is being healed.

In India they put a charm in a silver or gold plate, or keep a charm engraved upon stone or metal; and the very fact of realizing that he possesses something in the form of a charm that has a healing influence upon him becomes such a help to the believer that he feels that every moment of the day and night he has the healer with him, and that he is being healed.

As a gift is nothing without the giver, so a charm is nothing without a personality that gives confidence to the patient. Therefore a charm written by an ordinary person has no effect; the personality of the person who writes the charm should be impressive, his piety, his spirituality, his love, his kindness, should all help to make the charm that he gives valuable and effective.

## Magnetized Water

Water is the most responsive substance; it partakes of the colour and effect of everything. The magnetism that runs through the finger-tips enters into everything that a healer holds in his hands, and thus water can be charged with that electricity more than any other substance. Again, the breath that heals is powerful enough to produce an added life in all life-giving substances. Water especially, which is a most invigorating substance, partakes of life from the breath.

Among the ancient Hindus there was a custom of giving water as a benediction to guests, which is observed even now. A Brahmin will as a rule first offer water to his guest which means not only to quench the thirst, but is like giving life to the guest. The Persians have called the water of life *Ab-e Hayat*, and in many verses one finds this word. Among Sufis everywhere in the East there is a custom that the Shaikh gives a loaf of bread or a glass of water, milk, syrup, or buttermilk, or a fruit or some sweet, which is accepted as something that heals both mind and body. No doubt it is not only the effect of the breath or touch, it has also the power of mind with it, which is hidden as a soul in the substance which is its body.

## Healing by Breathing

A healer must know in the first place that breath is the very life, that breath is the giver of life, and that breath is the bringer of life. One can live without food for some time, but one cannot live without breath even for a few minutes. This shows that the sustenance that breath brings to man's life is much greater and much more important than any nourishment upon earth. Every atom of man's body is radiant; but if the body is the flame, the breath is the fire, and as the flame belongs to the fire, so the body belongs to the breath. As long as breath dwells in it, it lives, and when breath leaves it, it is dead, for all its beauty, strength, and complicated mechanism. That is why the effect of the breath of a holy person can magnetize water, bread, milk, or wine, fruit or flower.

The breath that is developed spiritually will have a healing effect upon any painful part that it falls upon. If one knows how to direct the breath there is no better process than healing with breath; and in all the different methods of healing breath is the main thing, since in breath is hidden the current of life.

## Healing by Magnetic Passes

All scriptures have explained in some way or other that life is like light. In the Moslem scripture the word *Nur* is used; in the Vedanta it is called *Chaitanya*. The nature of this light is to express itself in a particular direction, and that accounts for the face and back in our forms. At the same time the tendency of the light is to spread. This can be seen in the tendency of fire or of water to spread; air shows the same tendency, and also earth and all things on earth. A deep study of every form will show that the nature of life is to spread in four directions, for instance north, south, east, and west, or head, foot, right, and left.

Life and light have their centre in the centre of every form, but express themselves through the directions in which they spread. Therefore the power of the hand has been shown in ancient symbology. Hindus have pictured the divine incarnations with four hands; this means two hands of the mind and two hands of the body, and that when four hands work together the work is fully accomplished. This shows that in healing the hands are most important. The physical hands are needed to help the hands of the mind, and when thought is directed from the mind through the hand its power becomes double and its expression fuller.

Every atom of man's being, mental or physical, is radiant and throws its rays outward; these are life itself and give life. All illness is lack of life; and it needs life to be cured. The power of electricity has been discovered by the scientist, and he believes that it cures diseases when it is used for that purpose, but the mystic has discovered ages ago the power of this hidden electricity, the life of the mind and the life of the body, and he believes and knows that its application in healing is most beneficial. There are sores and wounds and painful parts which are too tender to touch. In such cases healing by magnetic passes, in other words by waving the hands over the affected part and so allowing thought to heal, brings about a successful cure.

### Healing by Touch

Every atom in man's body is in reality radiant, living and powerful compared with other objects, herbs, or drugs. By the very fact of being a living body, besides being the finest and most perfect compared with other living bodies, it has a great power. Therefore, shaking hands, speaking to a person and touching him have a certain effect. In India when a wrestler goes to a wrestling match and when he comes back his teacher pats him on the back, saying, 'Shabaz, Bravo!' This actually gives him added strength and courage and power which otherwise he would not have had. People speaking in friendship, and even disputing and arguing, hold each other's hands, which brings about a better understanding. A mother takes away the discomfort and restlessness of the child in one moment by patting it. Therefore massage is helpful when there is pain, and yet it is a poor treatment when compared with the healing treatment; for the healer operates the power of the mind through his fingers, as a musician produces his feelings on the violin. Is it everybody that can produce on the violin the same tone that an expert could? It is not the placing of the finger on a certain place on the instrument; it is the feeling of the musician's heart manifesting through his finger-tips that produces a living tone. So it is with the touch of a spiritual healer.

## Healing by Glance

The eye is the most wonderful and powerful factor in the body, which conveys to another pleasure or displeasure, joy or sorrow, love or hatred, without a word being spoken. This shows that the eye is the most responsive instrument for the mind to express thought and feeling. Sometimes in an assembly two people just look at each other and there is agreement between them, and two people may stare at each other and it may have a worse effect than shooting; this again proves that both fire and water can manifest either to destroy or to inspire. To a healer, therefore, there is no better means than the eyes to send his thought of healing; and there is no better means of receiving this thought in the patient than his eyes. The healer can send the healing power through his glance to the painful part of the body, but it is more helpful still when he sends his power direct to the eyes of the patient. As there is a link between the mind and the eyes of the healer who sends the power, so there is a link between the eyes and the mind of the patient who receives it. Medicine can touch the physical body, but thought can touch the mind, where the root of every disease often is;

and a suggestion that a powerful healer gives to his patient reaches his heart and destroys the germ of disease.

The eyes of every person are not capable of healing. It is the penetrating glance and stillness of the eyes, then the power of the glance and ability to aim, that are necessary. These are developed by certain exercises, though some eyes have a natural ability for this purpose. Also, concentration of mind which gives power is necessary in healing, for power of mind directed by the glance brings about a successful result.

## Healing by Suggestion

There are five elements that constitute man's being: earth, water, fire, air, and ether. Air represents the voice, and it reaches the ether, which means that the voice reaches farther than anything else in the world. It touches the depths of man's heart. Therefore music is a living miracle. There is nothing that can thrill man's being through and through as sound can. This explains why suggestion is much greater and more beneficial in healing than any other remedy.

In India, where the daily life of the people is based upon psychical laws, they take great care in speaking to another person that it may not produce a bad effect upon his physical, mental, or spiritual self. A healer, who by the power of Zikr develops the healing power of his voice, impresses his word with the power of his heart on the heart of the patient.

The healer must be sincere in his suggestions, because all the power lies in his sincerity; he must also be self-confident; he must have psychic power developed in him; but beyond and above all he must be a good man, so that at the time no thought of humiliation or of any sort of uneasiness should come to him. His thoughts, feelings, and actions should be satisfactory to his conscience; if not, any discomfort, dissatisfaction, fear, or repentance weakens his power. Then he is no longer capable of healing, however learned and powerful he may be. When the healer thinks he is healing, his power is as small as a drop; when he thinks God is healing, and when owing to this thought his own self is forgotten and he is only conscious of the self of God, then his power becomes as large as the ocean.

## Healing by Presence

There is warmth in fire, and there is a greater warmth in feeling. The presence of a person with warm feelings can create an atmosphere of warmth, and the presence of the cold-hearted can freeze one. No doubt warmth of heart is not the only quality the healer needs, he must have the power to heal, besides concentration and a desire to heal; but at the same time it is the name of Christ that is known as that of the Messiah. Messiah in the East means healer, and for a Messiah the power of love is the first quality, love in the form of sympathy. One sympathizes with another, thinking perhaps, 'He is my relation, friend, or acquaintance', but when sympathy develops to its fullest extent one begins to see in everybody 'I', 'myself', and the pain of everybody one begins to feel as one's own pain.

This is a sign of a true Messiah. How can he heal the wounds of the hearts of the children of the earth and relieve them from pains and sufferings, since life is full of them, when his sympathy is not awakened to such a degree that he feels the pain of another even before feeling his own pain? Every healer who has a spiritual aspiration must develop a spark of the fire of the heart of the Messiah; and then even before trying to heal a person his very presence will heal. When a child is ill the mother approaches it with the wish that it may be well, with a pain in her heart for the suffering of her child. From that moment she becomes a healer, her touch, her word, her glance do more than medicine or any other remedy. When this mother quality is developed in the heart of the healer, then, when he heals not for any return except the happiness of seeing a soul released from pain, he becomes a healer who can heal merely by his presence.

## Healing by Prayer

Prayer is a wonderful means of healing oneself and another, for concentration alone, without the thought of God, is powerless; it is the divine ideal which strengthens the healing power, which gives it a living spirit. Therefore a spiritual healer has more hope of success than a material healer. For the material healer directs his own thought; however powerful it may be it is limited by his own personality; but the spiritual healer who in the thought of God and His divine power forgets himself, has much greater success than the former. It does not matter what form of prayer one uses, sincere prayer in every form will bring a fruitful result.

Prayer is in reality the contemplation of God's presence, who is the power and origin of the whole creation; and it is considering oneself as nothing before Him, and placing the wish which stands before one's personality before the Almighty. Therefore naturally the result must be incomparably greater, though it depends upon the contemplation of every individual.

In the first place, he who prays for the cure of another must surely be blessed, because goodwill and love, from which his prayer rises, of necessity bring a blessing to him. Also prayer for one's own cure is not selfish, it is making oneself a fitting instrument to be more useful in the scheme of life. On the other hand, neglect of one's own health very often is a crime. Praying to God in thought is perhaps better than in speech, but it must be remembered that speech makes it concrete; therefore thought with speech makes prayer more effective than thought alone. Words without thought are vain repetitions.

## Absent Healing

When a healer has practised healing for a certain time success-fully, then the next step in the line of healing is to heal a patient from a distance. The method of absent healing is totally different from healing in the presence. In absent healing the power of thought alone is necessary, and those who are accustomed to use the magnetism through the tips of the fingers, through the eyes, through touch, find it difficult to direct their thought-power without an external channel. Also when the patient is not pre-sent, in the first place the beginner wonders whether his thought-power will reach the patient, and it is also difficult to hold in one's thought a patient who is not present.

The mastery of Fikr helps a healer to hold the thought of the patient before his mind, and it is Fikr that helps to heal a patient from a distance. Breath, so to speak, is an electric current that can be attached anywhere; distance makes no difference. A cur-rent of breath so established puts the ethereal waves in space into motion, and according to the healer's magnetic power the space between the healer and the patient becomes filled with a running current of healing power. There is no doubt that spiritual evolution is the first thing necessary; without this the mind power of a healer, however strong, is too feeble for the purpose.

By spiritual development is meant God-consciousness. There is a believer in God who may be called pious, but it is the God-conscious who become spiritual. It is the belief and realization that, 'I do not exist, but God', which gives power to the healer to heal from a distance; also it is this realization that gives him the belief that his thought can reach to any distance, because the knowledge of the all-pervading God gives him the realization that the Absolute is life in itself, and that even space, which means nothing to the average person, is everything; in fact, it is the very life of all things.

# 5
# Methods of Healing

## The Origin of Healing

CONSCIOUSLY or unconsciously every being is capable of healing himself or others. This instinct is inborn in insects, birds, and beasts, as well as in man. All these find their own medicine and heal themselves and each other in various ways. In ancient days the doctors and healers learned much from animals about the treatment of disease. This shows that natural intuition has manifested in the lower creation as well as in the higher. The scientists of today should not, therefore, claim with pride that they are the inventors of chemical remedies, but should humbly bow their heads in prayer, seeing that each atom of this universe, conscious of its sickness, procures for itself from within or without a means for its restoration. In other words, medicines were not discovered by physicians, but were intuitively found in creation as the necessity for them arose.

The excess of man's artificial remedies has had the effect of increasing disease. This is also mainly due to the modern artificial ways of life, so different from the natural living of the ancients which is ridiculed today by so-called civilization. Today the luxuries and needs of life are obtained at the sacrifice of true health and comfort.

Healing without drugs and medicines is the most natural method, although the absolute neglect of them is inadvisable. There are cases in which surgical instruments are also permissible but only when absolutely necessary. If horses can move wagons, why should engines be used? In the same way if a disease can be cured with a simple remedy the mental power should not be wasted, for it may be used in a more serious case. If every malady were to be healed mentally then why were all drugs and herbs created? On the other hand diseases which will yield more easily to mental treatment should not be left entirely to material remedies, for their root must first be healed. So many patients recover temporarily by the help of medicine but again become sick, and in such cases healing is especially needed. It is much to be deplored that in the present age such important work as healing has been undertaken by people who are often most materially minded and do not understand its psychology, making it a profession and thus bringing discredit upon it.

Self-healing is more desirable than healing by others; the former strengthens the will, the latter weakens it. Many people think that hypnotic and psychic power alone can heal; but they do not realize how the healer must first heal himself by the practice of the strictest morality from the lowest to the highest phase of his existence. He must purify himself by *Iman*, or faith. Then only can he claim to be a healer.

There are five kinds of disease caused by various disorders on different planes of existence. Some diseases on the physical plane are contracted from without, while others spring from within. There are several supposed causes, but in reality the true cause of disease is weakness, while the cause of health is strength. This does not mean physical weakness or strength only, but strength and weakness on all planes of existence. Activity causes what is called life, while the reverse brings about death, the former

causes circulation and the latter congestion. Circulation gives health, while congestion causes disease.

The scientists of today are giving electric treatment as a comparatively new discovery, and it is claimed that it is the most beneficial of all remedies. Healing is also electric treatment, and has been given throughout the different planes of life for ages. Every being has a natural gift of healing in a greater or lesser degree, but it may be developed. The physical and mental faculties should be opened in such a way that the electric vibrations on the various planes of existence are enabled to operate. Physical vibrations depend upon the purity and energy of the body, and they can be projected through the finer parts of the body such as the palms of the hands, the tips of the fingers, the soles of the feet, the cheek, the forehead, the ear, the lips, nose, and eyes. The finest of all these is the eye; it is much more useful than all the other organs, for it is through the eyes that the electric rays can be emitted. The nose has also an important part to perform, it being the very channel of breath. The ears can work when the healer is spiritually advanced, and the vibrations can also pass through the tips of the fingers.

The Oriental custom of placing the eyes upon the holy hands or feet of the sage is not only expressive of humility, but it has a still greater meaning. It signifies the healing by the holy hands or feet which illuminate the devotee. The sages who bless these aspiring souls by placing their hands upon the head, inspire them by sending forth the rays of their power through the finger-tips. In kissing the hands or feet of the Holy Ones the Orientals have the same object in view. In the same way the caress of the mother heals the child of all its pains and soothes it to sleep. Courage and consolation are given to another by placing the hands on his shoulders, the vibrations in this action give new life and courage.

# Physical Healing

A patient can only be healed if he has sufficient faith in the power of healing and confidence in the healer. In the case of self-healing, self-confidence and the power of breath and concentration are most necessary. There is a well-known story that Shams-e Tabrèz, the Shiva of Persia, was once most respectfully entreated by the priests of the day to awaken the crown prince, who had just died, from his last long sleep. The Shah, his father, issued a decree that if there was any truth at all in religion his only son must be restored to life by prayer, otherwise all the mosques would be destroyed and the mullahs be put to the sword. In order to save many lives Shams-e Tabrèz complied with their request and sought the dead body of the prince. He first said to the body of the prince, 'Kun ba Ismi Allah' (Awake at the call of God). The dead body did not move. He then, under the spell of ecstasy, exclaimed, 'Kun ba Ismi" (Awake at my command). At this suggestion the prince immediately arose. The story goes on to relate that this abrupt command, although it restored the prince to life, brought the charge that he had claimed to be God against Shams-e Tabrèz, and according to the religious law, he was condemned to be flayed alive. He gladly submitted to this punishment in order to keep religion intact, as it is the only means of elevating the multitude.

By this we understand that Shams-e Tabrèz in his first suggestion to the dead spoke conventionally, entreating God as a third person, which had not the slightest effect on the dead body; but in his next command he lost his individual self from his consciousness and felt himself to be the whole Being of God. This story makes it clear that the healer must be confident of his at-oneness with God, and during the time of healing he should most assuredly feel the power of the Almighty working through him, thus absolutely losing the thought of his individual self.

The electric battery which heals is charged in three ways: by controlling the breath, by strengthening the will, and by absorbing the electricity of the sphere.

In order to make use of this healing battery it is most essential that the eyes should be made to work so that they project the electricity. They must be first cured of their nervousness, that ever moving condition to which they are addicted from birth. The eyes are naturally weakened and made tired by allowing them to respond from morning to night, to every attraction which invites their attention. The healer, in order to make use of them for healing, first trains them to be steady.

The electricity can be absorbed by striking with the fingers the finer vibrations in space; and it can be discharged in the same way by slowly passing the tips of the fingers through the space above the affected part of the patient's body. Sometimes passing the fingers closer to the body, and sometimes slightly touching the affected part is helpful. It depends upon the intensity of pain suffered by the patient and the amount of electricity required. It is very necessary that each time the fingers have passed over the affected part they should be shaken in order to disperse the poisons collected there; in other words the poisonous germs collected on the fingers should be thrown away. It is advisable to shake the fingers over a fire so that the germs may not be left on the floor, and also to have incense burning in the room. Some healers, in order to protect the fingers, make use of peacock feathers, which sweep away all such germs.

The healer can test his healing power by feeling the electric current running through his fingers as he shakes them. A healer even when playing an instrument can heal the listeners with his music. If a healer gives a gift with a good wish it brings good luck, and if he writes a word it becomes a charm, a healer in itself which heals the possessor and keeps him free from death and disaster.

## Mental Healing

Mental healing is performed by suggestion. In most cases the parents are the first healers, for they convey their thought to the child by the knitting of the brow or by looking at him fixedly. Even animals can be trained in the same way.

There are many diseases of the human mind produced by self-consciousness. They develop unconsciously, and are such as love of praise and flattery, intolerance of insult, irritability, infatuation, jealousy, anger, passion, and greed, besides the craving for alcohol and drugs. In order to cure such diseases the healer must have great control over himself, or his own shortcomings may keep the patient back. The Holy Prophet was once requested by an aged woman to speak to her son, who spent all his daily wage on dates, leaving her penniless. The Prophet promised to do so after five weeks' interval. On the appointed day the boy was brought before the Prophet, who spoke to him very kindly, saying, 'You are such a sensible lad that you ought to remember that your mother has endured much suffering for your sake, sacrificing all her wages in order to bring you up; and now she is so old and you are in a position to support her, and you are squandering your money on dates. Is this just or right? I hope by the grace and mercy of Allah you will give up this habit.' The boy listened very attentively and profited by what he heard. But the disciples of the Prophet wondered, and asked why the reproof was delayed for thirty-five days. The Holy Prophet explained, saying, 'I myself am fond of dates, and I felt that I had no right to advise the lad to abstain from them until I had myself refrained from eating them for five weeks.' The healer of character should never for a single moment try to heal another of weaknesses to which he is himself addicted.

## Spiritual Healing

Spiritual healing is still higher in its nature than either of the former methods. It can be performed by a single being as well as by a group of people. In this case the heart of the healer can send forth its feelings and vibrations, and in accordance with their intensity the subject is healed. In absent spiritual healing the desire spreads forth its rays and reaches the patient wherever he may be, curing him without the presence of the healer. The concentration of several people united together works still more wonderfully.

The power of the healer depends upon the warmth of his heart. Devotees by their power of concentration, by their purity of life, and by their divine love become wonderful healers; their every tear and sigh become a source of healing for themselves and those around them. Devotion is the fire in which all infirmities are consumed, and the devotee becomes illuminated within himself; and the joy of the devotee and his pain cannot possibly be compared with any other joy in life. Spiritual healing does not require the fixed gaze, the touch of the fingers, or the power of breath, but Tawajoh (a kind glance), or Do'a (a good thought) of the spiritual healer serves the purpose.

## Abstract Healing

In abstract healing the soul, heart, and body are healed of all diseases and weaknesses therein. This healing is only possible during the ecstasy of the healer. The strong psychical vibrations which run through the pores of his body from his inner self naturally pierce through the bodies, hearts, and souls of all around him, who receive them in accordance with their power of receptivity. Murshids have frequently inspired their mureeds without reading or discussing, and such mureeds have reached perfection. It is a wonderful phenomenon which an exceptional mureed once in a while experiences under the guidance of his Murshid.

There is a story told of Hafiz Shirazi, who, together with ten other Hafiz, was being trained under the same Murshid. A certain time was set apart for their meditation and other practices, and a certain time for food and sleep. Hafiz Shirazi kept awake during the night in rapt contemplation of Allah. After years of patient waiting, one evening the Murshid in ecstasy called for Hafiz. The wakeful Hafiz was the only one who heard, and he answered the call and was blessed by the Murshid, who chose this ideal time to inspire all his mureeds. Each time he called for Hafiz the same Hafiz answered the call, all the others being asleep. So the wakeful one received an elevenfold blessing, his own and that of the ten others who lost this precious opportunity by their sleep. And Hafiz became the greatest spiritual healer of his time, whose every word, from that day to this, has been powerful to heal.